Mad about Plaid!

Mad about Plaid!

Quilts from Classic Fabrics

DEBBIE BACON

Martingale®
& COMPANY

Mad about Plaid! Quilts from Classic Fabrics

© 2004 by Debbie Bacon

That Patchwork Place® is an
imprint of Martingale & Company®.

Martingale & Company
20205 144th Avenue NE
Woodinville, WA 98072-8478
www.martingale-pub.com

Printed in China
09 08 07 06 05 04   8 7 6 5 4 3 2 1

Library of Congress Cataloging-in-Publication Data

Bacon, Debbie.
  Mad about plaid! : quilts from classic fabrics /
Debbie Bacon.
    p. cm.
  ISBN 1-56477-518-6
 1. Quilting—Patterns. 2. Patchwork—Patterns.
3. Plaid. I. Title.
  TT835 .B225 2004
  746 .46041—dc22
                                    2003021712

MISSION STATEMENT

*Dedicated to providing quality products
and service to inspire creativity.*

CREDITS

President: Nancy J. Martin

CEO: Daniel J. Martin

Publisher: Jane Hamada

Editorial Director: Mary V. Green

Managing Editor: Tina Cook

Technical Editor: Karen Costello Soltys

Copy Editor: Liz McGehee

Design Director: Stan Green

Illustrator: Brian Metz

Cover and Text Designer: Regina Girard

Photographer: Brent Kane

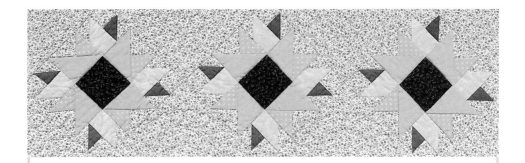

DEDICATION

To my beloved husband, Ron, who puts up with
my mess and applauds my efforts.

ACKNOWLEDGMENTS

I'd like to express my humble appreciation for
the family and friends who encouraged me
to do the work, especially:

Charlene Kimball, for being the best
mother-in-law and hand quilter,

Mary Covey, for her wisdom and
delightful machine quilting,

Sheryl Miller, for her
beautiful machine quilting, and

the dear Lord, for keeping his promises.

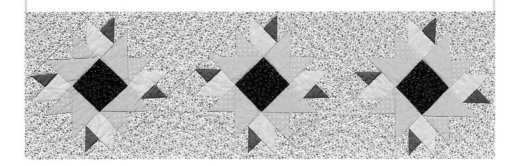

Contents

A Pondering of Plaids

When you think of plaids, what comes to mind? Tartans, madras, or homespun cottons? Maybe it's your family's 1970s-era sofa!

You might be surprised to learn that plaids are as ancient as the technique of weaving itself. Even though the looms used today seem complex, the basic process of weaving fabric is simple. Warp threads are strung on a loom, and weft threads are woven under and over the warp to produce cloth. Variations in colored threads create the designs.

A Little Bit of Background

Recent discoveries in western China of 4,000-year-old mummies with remarkably well-preserved prehistoric woolen textiles finally give us insights into the weaves, colors, and designs of the textiles. In her book *The Mummies of Urumchi,* author Elizabeth Wayland Barber, one of the world's leading scholars on ancient textiles, describes in great detail the conditions of these mummies and their garments. A surprising discovery is that their woolen clothes, which rarely would survive more than a few centuries under normal circumstances, have been preserved so well that the colors are as bright and clear as if they had just been woven. These mummies are wearing woolen clothes woven in a pattern we would recognize at once: tartan plaid.

The term "tartan" is derived from *tiretaine,* a French word for a type of woolen fabric. Archaeological evidence shows us that the Celts have been weaving plaid textiles—or tartans—for at least 3,000 years. In fact, the Bronze and Iron Age ancestors of the historic Celts wore woolen plaid cloth that is almost identical to modern examples. The main difference is that the ancient plaids contain no more than two or three colors, while the modern tartans are often multicolored.

Tartan Plaids

Another group of notable and instantly recognizable plaids are madras plaids. These bright and colorful fabrics originated in Madras (now Chennai), India, about 1830, where they were woven of silk or cotton and worn as turbans. Madras fabrics today are finely woven shirting and dress fabrics with varied designs or plaids in bright colors as well as white. Often the dyes used for madras plaids are not colorfast, and each time the fabric or garment is washed the colors bleed a bit, changing the look of the fabric and softening the lines between the color changes.

Madras Plaids

Classic homespun plaids also have a place in history. Today we use the term homespun to categorize a large group of cotton plaids familiar to quilters. However, homespun is a term used since the early 1600s to describe fabric woven at home from homespun fibers. The fibers could have been linen, wool, or cotton, and the fabrics were generally loosely woven. The fabric was used to make clothes, bedding, and whatever else was needed around the colonial home. Homespun can be plain—made from undyed fibers—or woven in a small-scale,

even, plaid pattern. These plaids were usually woven in two colors.

Homespun Plaids

Today, it's common to find printed plaids in quilt shops too. These plaids have a definite right and wrong side, as the plaid design is not created by weaving different colored threads over and under one another. Instead, the colors are printed on the surface of the fabric. With this type of plaid, you might find that the lines are intentionally squiggly or that small motifs, such as dots, have been added to the design. While the history of printed plaids doesn't travel back quite so far, it's fun to incorporate this type of fabric into your quiltmaking repertoire.

Printed Plaids

Plaids Have Personality

Each plaid has its own characteristics, whether it's a tartan, madras, homespun—or something in between. Some plaids are more eye-catching, while others tend to recede and blend in. Some plaids are very intricate in design, while others are a bit more soothing and simple.

The most amazing thing is that plaids never seem to grow old. Other prints used for quilting may come and go, but plaids remain timeless. The colors and patterns used can elicit a feeling or a mood. A red-and-green plaid may remind you of Christmas, while brightly colored madras plaids look refreshing in the hot summer. Homespuns tend to exude a warm and snuggly feeling. These moods can be mixed when combining plaids to add interest and texture.

One of the key considerations when choosing a plaid is its color. However, some quilters may be baffled by the line element in the fabric. Do you try to match the lines? Or worry if they're cut slightly off-grain? The answer, perhaps, lies within your own personality. Some quiltmakers like their work to have a more formal look, and in that case, cutting plaids exactly on grain will be more satisfying.

On the other hand, if you're a quiltmaker who likes things a little less formal, leaning more to a primitive style, you probably won't be as likely to worry if the grain line isn't exact. The eye will naturally follow a line until it ends, and if the line is not straight or is broken, the eye seeks the next line to follow, which promotes a movement through the design. To make a design even more interesting for the eye to comprehend, try cutting plaids on the bias as I did in "Plaid Pineapple" on page 33 and for the borders of "Sunflowers" on page 18. As noted quiltmaker and author Roberta Horton of Berkley, California, once wrote, "If a quilt needs to be structured and controlled to be effective, then plaids and stripes should be used on-grain. If a quilt needs some vitality and life, one way to accomplish that is to work off-grain with directional fabrics." I couldn't agree with her more!

When making a project with lines going every which way, controlling the plaids can seem like a challenge. Part of the control comes from the type of patchwork block you are using. Another way to control the quilt or to give the eyes a place to rest is to add a calming frame to the quilt. Using a solid or subtle print fabric for a border will contain the busyness of the plaids. But too much solid fabric can overwhelm a project and become too heavy. To keep the values in the center involved throughout a project, bring some of the qualities inside the solid border to the outer borders. For instance, consider using a narrow inner border that is quite plain, but then add a plaid outer border that will blend the values and complement the quilt center.

I hope you'll enjoy making the projects in this book and discover that working with plaids can be quite fun, whether you mix them with other quilting fabrics or go for broke and use nothing but plaids as in "Shadow Plaid" on page 13. You'll soon discover that plaids are quite easy to get along with!

Quilt
Projects

Shadow Plaid

Finished Quilt Size: 77" x 88" ◆ Finished Block Size: 18" x 18"

"The more the merrier" has always been my philosophy when working on scrap quilts. My stitch group loved this project so much that we traded plaid bias squares to add to the variety of colors and values we each already owned. The key to this design is the value placement of the plaids. Some of them are a little tricky to figure out, but a colored lens, such as a Ruby Beholder, can help you determine their relative color values.

MATERIALS

Yardages are based on 42"-wide fabrics.

- ¼ yard *each* of 36 different dark plaids or striped fabrics
- ¼ yard *each* of 24 different light plaids or striped fabrics
- ¼ yard *each* of 12 different medium plaids or striped fabrics
- ¾ yard of red plaid fabric for outer border
- ½ yard of red checked fabric for second border
- ¼ yard of black fabric for first border
- 5½ yards of backing fabric
- 1 yard of black check fabric for binding
- 84" x 95" piece of batting
- Optional: 1 roll of 3"-finished triangle-square paper

CUTTING

From the medium plaid fabrics, cut:
72 squares, 3⅞" x 3⅞"; cut squares once diagonally to yield 144 triangles

From the dark plaid fabrics, cut:
216 squares, 3⅞" x 3⅞"; cut squares once diagonally to yield 432 triangles

From the light plaid fabrics, cut:
144 squares, 3⅞" x 3⅞", cut squares once diagonally to yield 288 triangles

From the black fabric, cut:
8 border strips, 1½" x 42"

From the red checked fabric, cut:
8 border strips, 2½" x 42"

From the red plaid fabric, cut:
9 border strips, 3½" x 42"

From the black checked fabric, cut:
2½"-wide bias strips, enough to yield 340" of binding

Making the Blocks

1. With right sides together, sew each medium plaid triangle to a dark plaid triangle along their long edges to make 144 bias squares. Press the seams toward the dark fabric. Trim to 3½" square. With right sides together, sew the light plaid triangles to the remaining dark plaid triangles along their long edges to make 288 bias squares. Press and trim the dog ears from the squares and check to be sure they each measure 3½" square.

   Note: It helps to keep the bias squares separated in sandwich bags by value: medium-dark and light-dark.

2. Each block is made of four quadrants. For each quadrant, you'll need three medium-dark bias squares and six light-dark bias squares. Referring to the diagram, arrange the bias squares into a nine-patch unit.

   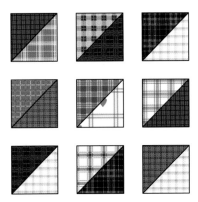

3. Double-check to make sure each bias square is positioned correctly, and then sew the bias squares together into rows. Press. Sew the three rows together to form the nine-patch unit. Press.

4. Repeat steps 2 and 3 to make three more quadrants, mixing up the color combinations but still using three medium-dark and six light-dark bias squares per block. Sew the four quadrants together with the light sections meeting in the middle, forming a diamond design. Press. Repeat to make 12 of these blocks. You will have leftover bias squares, which will be used for the borders.

   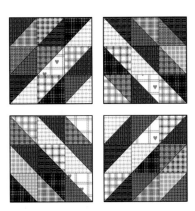

   Make 12.

Assembling the Quilt

1. Referring to the assembly diagram and the quilt photograph on page 13, arrange the blocks in four rows of three blocks each. Sew the blocks together. Press. Sew the rows together. Press.

Assembly Diagram

2. With the leftover bias squares, make two strips, with 24 bias squares each, to frame the sides of the quilt top. Follow the illustration carefully for placement of the dark triangles.

Make 2.

3. Sew the strips to the sides of the quilt top so that the edge with the light triangles is pointing toward the center of the quilt top on each side.

Adding the Borders

1. Sew the 1½"-wide black border strips together in pairs. Measure the width of the quilt top and trim two of the black border strips to this length, which should be approximately 60½". Sew the borders to the quilt top and bottom and press the seams toward the borders.

2. Measure the length of the quilt top and trim the remaining two black border strips to this length, which should be approximately 74½". Sew these borders to the sides of the quilt and press the seams toward the borders.

3. For the second border, sew the 2½"-wide red checked fabric strips together in pairs. Measure the width of the quilt top again, and trim two of the border strips to this measurement (approximately 62½"). Sew these border strips to the top and bottom of the quilt in the same manner as for the first border.

4. Measure the length of the quilt and trim the remaining two red checked border strips to this length (approximately 78½"). Sew them to the sides of the quilt as before.

5. For the pieced border, set aside four bias squares for the corners. Use the remaining bias squares to make 48 sets of flying-geese units, where the light sides of the triangles form a larger triangle in the center of the unit.

 Reserve 4 for corners.   Make 48.

6. Sew 11 flying-geese units together side by side to form the top and bottom borders. Sew the borders to the quilt top with the dark triangles in the seam. As a result, the white triangles will be pointing toward the quilt center. Press the seams toward the red checked borders.

7. Sew 13 flying-geese units together to form the side borders. Add one corner bias square to each end of each border, so that the dark triangle will be joined to these border strips and to the adjacent borders once the borders are attached. Sew the strips to the sides of the quilt top and press the seams toward the red checked borders.

Make 2.

8. For the outer border, sew the 3½"-wide red plaid strips together in four sets of two strips each. Cut the remaining strip in half and sew one piece to two of the sets. Measure the quilt through the center and trim the two shorter strips to this length (approximately 66½"). Sew the strips to the top and bottom of the quilt. Press the seams toward the red plaid borders.

9. Measure the length of the quilt and trim the two longer red strips to this length (approximately 88½"). Sew these strips to the sides of the quilt and press the seams toward the red plaid borders.

Quilt Plan

Finishing the Quilt

1. Piece the quilt backing and trim it so that it is approximately 6" larger than the quilt top.

2. Layer the quilt top, batting, and backing; baste the layers together.

3. Hand or machine quilt as desired. The quilt shown was quilted by hand, ¼" from the seam allowances, to enhance the diamond shape.

4. Trim the excess batting and backing ¼" from the outer edges.

5. Sew the 2½"-wide black check bias strips together to make bias binding. Attach the binding to your quilt, referring to page 76.

6. If desired, add a label to your quilt.

Sunflowers

Finished Quilt Size: 47" x 47" ◆ Finished Block Size: 9" x 9"

After a long and gray winter, it is such a blessing when the daffodils
and forsythia of spring bring a promise of the summer to come.
Seeking to bring their cheerful yellows into the house, I made
a quilt to brighten any room and chase the grays away.

MATERIALS

Yardages are based on 42"-wide fabrics.

◆ 2 yards of light print for background

◆ 1½ yards of white-and-navy blue plaid for outer border (cut on bias)

◆ 1 yard of navy blue plaid for inner border (cut on bias)

◆ ¼ yard of dark yellow print for sunflowers

◆ ¼ yard of medium yellow print for sunflowers

◆ ¼ yard of light yellow print for sunflowers

◆ ⅛ yard of brown print for flower centers

◆ ⅛ yard of green solid for leaves

◆ 3 yards of backing fabric

◆ ⅝ yard of yellow print for flat piping and binding

◆ 50" x 50" square of batting

CUTTING

From the green solid fabric, cut:

2 strips, 2¼" x 42"; crosscut strips into 18 squares, 2½" x 2½". Cut squares once diagonally to yield 36 triangles.

From the light background print, cut:

5 strips, 2" x 42"; crosscut strips into 72 squares, 2½" x 2½"

2 strips, 2½" x 42"; crosscut strips into 18 squares, 2½" x 2½". Cut squares once diagonally to yield 36 triangles.

1 strip, 4¼" x 42"; crosscut into 9 squares, 4¼" x 4¼". Cut squares twice diagonally to yield 36 triangles.

2 squares, 14½" x 14½"; cut squares twice diagonally to yield 8 setting triangles

2 squares, 10" x 10"; cut squares once diagonally to yield 4 corner triangles

From the light yellow print, cut:

3 strips, 2" x 42"; crosscut into 36 rectangles, 2" x 3½"

From the medium yellow print, cut:

1 strip, 4¼" x 42"; crosscut strip into 9 squares, 4¼" x 4¼". Cut squares twice diagonally to yield 36 triangles.

From the dark yellow print, cut:

2 strips, 3⅞" x 42"; crosscut strips into 18 squares, 3⅞" x 3⅞". Cut squares once diagonally to yield 36 triangles.

From the brown print, cut:

1 strip, 3½" x 42"; crosscut strip into 9 squares, 3½" x 3½"

From the navy plaid, cut *on the bias:*

2 border strips, 1½" x 40"

2 border strips, 1½" x 42"

From the white-and-navy plaid, cut *on the bias:*

2 border strips, 4½" x 42"

2 border strips, 4½" x 50"

From the yellow print for binding, cut:

4 piping strips, 1" x 42"

5 binding strips, 2½" x 42"

Making the Blocks

The Sunflower blocks are made of two different pieced units, A and B, as well as a center brown square.

Unit A

1. Sew together a 2½" green and a 2½" light print triangle, right sides together. Press the seams toward the green fabric. Trim the completed bias squares to 2" square. Repeat to make a total of 36 bias squares.

2. Join the bias squares to the 2" background squares, paying careful attention to the color placement. Press the seam allowance toward the background square.

3. To form the other half of the corner units, sew a 2½" light print square to one end of a 2" x 3½" light yellow rectangle, using a diagonal seam as shown. First, fold the light squares in half diagonally and finger-press the crease to mark your stitching line. Then open up the square and place it right sides together on one end of the rectangle, making sure to position the diagonal crease as shown.

4. Stitch along the diagonal crease. Flip up the inside corner of the square, folding it back on itself to match the outer corner of the unit. Trim away the excess fabric that lies beneath the triangle, leaving a ¼" seam allowance. Press.

5. Sew the rectangle unit to the bias-square unit along their long edges to form a 3½" pieced square. Repeat to make a total of 36 of these A units, four for each block.

Unit A
Make 36.

Unit B

1. Join the 4¼" light print and medium yellow triangles together in pairs as shown. Press the seams toward the medium yellow fabric and trim the dog ears. Repeat to make 36 of these pieced triangles.

Make 36.

2. With right sides together, join the 3⅞" dark yellow triangles to the pieced triangles along their long edges to form a pieced square. Press the seams toward the dark yellow fabric. Make 36 of unit B.

Unit B
Make 36.

Block Assembly

1. Lay out the block in three rows, using the 3½" brown squares for the block centers.

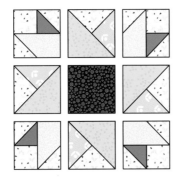

2. Join the units together in rows and then join the rows together. Press. Repeat to make a total of nine blocks.

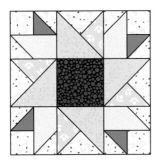

Sunflower Block
Make 9.

Assembling the Quilt

1. Referring to the quilt assembly diagram and the quilt photograph on page 18, arrange the Sunflower blocks, the setting triangles, and the corner triangles in diagonal rows. Sew the blocks and triangles together in rows and press the seams toward the setting triangles.

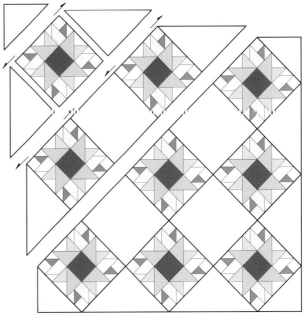

Quilt Assembly

2. Sew the rows together and press the seams toward the setting pieces. Add the corner triangles and press the seams toward these triangles. Trim away the excess fabric from the corners and sides with a rotary cutter and ruler to square up the quilt top.

Adding the Borders

The inner and outer borders are cut on the bias, so take care not to stretch them when pinning and sewing them to your quilt top.

1. Measure the length of your quilt top and trim the two shortest navy plaid border strips to this measurement. Sew them to the sides of the quilt. Press the seams toward the borders.

2. Measure the width of the quilt top and trim the remaining two navy plaid border strips to this measurement. Sew them to the top and bottom of the quilt, and press the seams toward the borders.

3. Fold the four 1"-wide yellow piping strips in half lengthwise and press. Measure the width and the length of the quilt top (they should both be approximately 39½"), and trim the four strips to this measurement. Matching the raw edges of the strip with one edge of the quilt top, machine baste a folded strip to the navy plaid border using a scant ¼" seam allowance. Baste the three other prepared strips in the same manner.

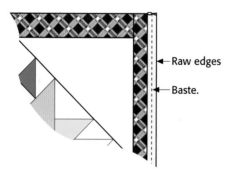

←— Raw edges

←— Baste.

4. Trim two of the 4½"-wide white-and-navy plaid border strips to fit the length of your quilt (approximately 39½"). Sew the border strips to the sides of the quilt. Press the seams toward the outer borders.

5. Measure the width of the quilt top and trim the remaining white-and-navy plaid border strips to this measurement (approximately 47½"). Sew these strips to the top and bottom of the quilt and press the seams toward the outer borders.

Quilt Plan

Finishing the Quilt

1. Piece the quilt backing and trim it so that it is approximately 6" larger than the quilt top.

2. Layer the quilt top, batting, and backing; baste the layers together.

3. Hand or machine quilt as desired. The quilt shown was quilted by hand, with feathered wreaths in the plain setting squares. The border was quilted along the lines of the plaid to create crosshatching.

4. Trim the excess batting and backing fabric ¼" from the outside edge.

5. Using the 2½"-wide yellow strips, make and attach the binding.

6. If desired, add a hanging sleeve and label your quilt.

Churn Dash

Finished Quilt Size: 70½" x 86½" ◆ Finished Block Size: 6" x 6"

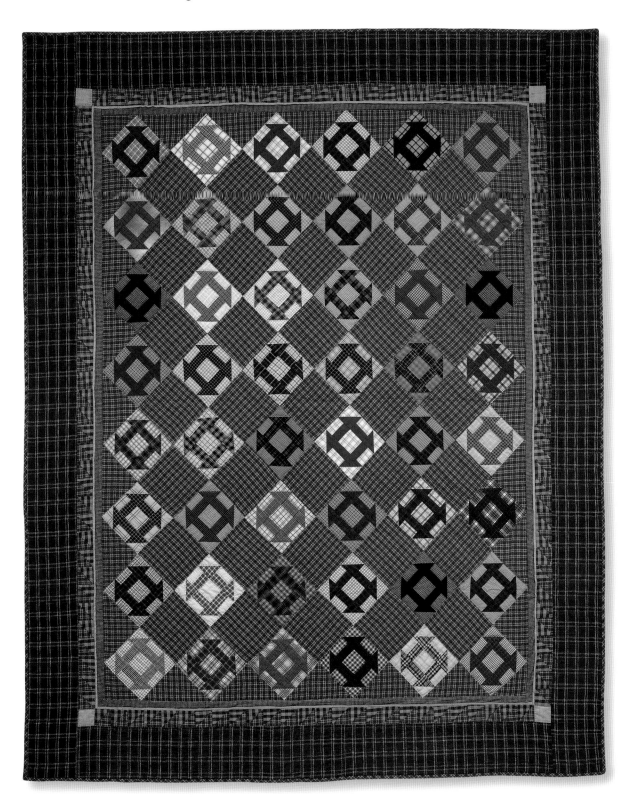

It is so much fun to trade blocks with quilting friends; if you've never tried it, I highly
recommend participating in an exchange. The variety of fabrics and the challenge of
a good trade usually spur you on to the best new ideas. The blocks in this Churn Dash
quilt are the result of a trade with new friends I met on the Internet. Someday,
we all plan to get together and see how the blocks became unique quilts.

MATERIALS

Yardages are based on 42"-wide fabrics.

◆ 3½ yards of red plaid for setting squares and triangles, border triangles, and bias binding

◆ 1¾ yards of green plaid for outer border

◆ ¼ yard *each* of 24 light plaids for blocks

◆ ⅛ yard *each* of 24 dark plaids for blocks

◆ ½ yard of green-and-tan plaid for border triangles

◆ ½ yard of small-scale green check for inner border

◆ ½ yard of small-scale yellow check for flat piping and corner squares

◆ 5⅛ yards of backing fabric

◆ 77" x 93" piece of batting

CUTTING

From *each* light plaid, cut:

4 squares, 3" x 3"; cut squares once diagonally to yield 8 triangles (192 total)

2 squares, 2½" x 2½" (48 total)

8 rectangles, 1½" x 2½" (192 total)

From *each* dark plaid, cut

4 squares, 3" x 3"; cut squares once diagonally to yield 8 triangles (192 total)

8 rectangles, 1½" x 2½" (192 total)

From the red plaid fabric, cut:

6 strips, 6½" x 42"; crosscut strips into 35 setting squares, 6½" x 6½"

2 strips, 9" x 42"; crosscut strips into 6 squares, 9" x 9". Cut squares twice diagonally to yield 24 setting triangles

2 squares, 7⅞" x 7⅞"; cut squares once diagonally to yield 4 corner triangles

5 strips, 3" x 42"; crosscut strips into 62 squares, 3" x 3". Cut squares once diagonally to yield 124 triangles.

2½"-wide bias strips, enough to yield 312" of binding

From the green-and-tan plaid fabric, cut:

5 strips, 3" x 42"; crosscut strips into 62 squares, 3" x 3". Cut squares once diagonally to yield 124 triangles.

From the small-scale green check, cut:

3 border strips, 1½" x 42"

4 border strips, 2" x 42"

From the small-scale yellow check, cut:

7 strips, 1½" x 42"

4 squares, 2½" x 2½"

From the green plaid, cut:

8 border strips, 6½" x 42"

Making the Blocks

For each block, use matching light and matching dark pieces. You should have enough of each light and each dark plaid fabric to make two blocks. Of course, you can mix and match the light and dark fabrics so that no two blocks are exactly the same.

1. Sew a dark plaid triangle to a light plaid triangle with right sides together. Repeat to make four matching triangle squares. Press the seam toward the dark plaid and trim the unit to 2½" square.

Make 4 per block.

2. Sew a dark plaid rectangle to a light plaid rectangle, right sides together. Press the seams toward the dark plaid. Repeat to make four identical 2½" strip squares.

Make 4 per block.

3. Lay out the block in rows, using the triangle squares, strip squares, and a plain, light plaid center square.

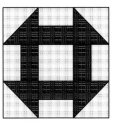

4. Sew the pieces together into rows. Press the seams in opposite directions from one row to another. Sew the rows together and press the block.

5. Repeat steps 1 through 4 to make a total of 48 blocks.

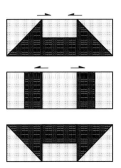

Churn Dash Block
Make 48.

Assembling the Quilt

1. Referring to the assembly diagram below and the quilt photograph on page 23, arrange the Churn Dash blocks in diagonal rows, alternating them with the red plaid setting squares and setting triangles.

2. Sew the blocks and setting pieces together into rows. Press the seams toward the setting squares and triangles.

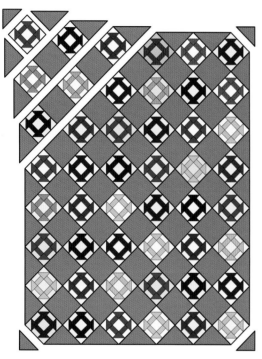

Quilt Assembly

3. Sew the rows together and press all seams in one direction.

4. Add the corner triangles and press. Trim away the excess fabric from the corner and side setting triangles using your rotary cutter and a long ruler. To do so, align the ¼" marking line with the intersection of the blocks and setting triangles to allow for the ¼" seam allowance.

Adding the Borders

1. Measure the width of your quilt. Sew the three 1½"-wide green check strips together end to end. From this long strip, cut two border strips the width of your quilt, which should be approximately 51½". Sew the strips to the top and bottom of the quilt and press the seam allowances toward the green check fabric.

2. Sew the four 2"-wide green check strips together end to end in pairs. Measure the length of your quilt and trim each of the long strips to this measurement, which should be approximately 70½". Sew these strips to the sides of the quilt and press the seam allowances toward the green borders.

3. Join the 1"-wide yellow strips together as you did for the green check strips: one set of three strips joined end to end, and two sets of two strips sewn together. Fold each long strip in half lengthwise and press.

4. Measure the width of your quilt top, and from the longest yellow strip cut two pieces to this measurement, which should be approximately 54½". Machine baste these folded strips to the inner border, aligning the raw edges and using a scant ¼" seam allowance.

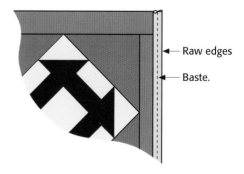

5. Measure the length of your quilt and trim the remaining two yellow strips to this measurement, which should be approximately 70½". Machine baste these strips to the sides of the quilt in the same manner as for the top and bottom strips.

6. Sew the 3" red plaid and green-and-tan plaid triangles together to make 124 triangle squares. Press all seams toward the darker triangles. Trim the completed triangle squares to 2½" x 2½".

7. Sew the triangle squares together into two strips of 27 triangle squares each for the top and bottom borders. Make two strips of 35 triangle squares each for the side borders. Press all seam allowances in the same direction.

8. Sew the shorter triangle-square borders to the top and bottom of the quilt with the green-and-tan triangles facing the inner border.

9. Sew a 2½" yellow check square to each end of the longer triangle-square borders and then sew these borders to the sides of the quilt, again with the green-and-tan triangles facing the inner border. Press all seams toward the inner border.

10. Sew three of the 6½"-wide green plaid outer border strips together end to end. Measure the width of your quilt and cut two border strips to this measurement, which should be approximately 58½". Sew these strips to the top and bottom of the quilt and press the seams toward the outer border.

11. Sew the remaining five 6½"-wide green plaid strips together end to end. Measure the length of your quilt and cut two border strips to this measurement, which should be approximately 86½". Sew these strips to the sides of the quilt and press the seams toward the outer border.

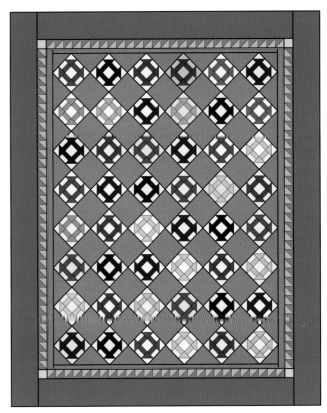

Quilt Plan

Finishing the Quilt

1. Piece the quilt backing and trim it so that it is approximately 6" larger than the quilt top.

2. Layer the quilt top, batting, and backing; baste the layers together.

3. Hand or machine quilt as desired. The quilt shown was quilted in the ditch by hand. The outer borders were quilted with straight lines, following the lines of the plaid fabric.

4. Trim the excess batting and backing fabric ¼" from the outside edge.

5. Using the 2½"-wide red plaid strips, make and attach the bias binding.

6. If desired, add a label to your quilt.

Celebration

Finished Quilt Size: 27½" x 32" ◆ Finished Block Size: 4½" x 4½"

*If you like to display the red, white, and blue, here's a patriotic little quilt for you!
The navy and red Ohio Star blocks are made from assorted woven and printed
plaids as well as some starry prints. I made this quilt during the time of the first
Gulf War to honor and support our servicemen and -women. Why not make this
small quilt for a banner to welcome guests to your next summertime celebration
or as an indoor wall hanging to show your colors anytime of the year?*

Materials

Yardages are based on 42"-wide fabrics.

◆ ⅛ yard *each* of 10 navy blue prints and plaids for stars

◆ ⅛ yard *each* of 10 red prints and plaids for stars

◆ 1⅛ yard of light print for background

◆ ½ yard of navy blue print for corner blocks and binding

◆ ⅜ yard of red print for border

◆ 1 yard of backing fabric

◆ 34" x 38" piece of batting

Cutting

From *each* navy print or plaid, cut:

2 squares, 2¾" x 2¾" (20 total)

1 square, 2" x 2" (10 total)

From the navy print for corner blocks and binding, cut:

8 squares, 2¾" x 2¾"

1 strip, 2" x 42"; crosscut strip into 16 squares, 2" x 2"

3 binding strips, 2½" x 42"

From *each* red print or plaid, cut:

2 squares, 2¾" x 2¾" (20 total)

1 square, 2" x 2" (10 total)

From the red print for border, cut:

4 border strips, 2" x 42"

From the light background print, cut:

4 strips, 2¾" x 42"; crosscut strips into 48 squares, 2¾" x 2¾"

4 strips, 2" x 42"; crosscut strips into 80 squares, 2" x 2"

8 border strips, 2" x 42"

Making the Blocks

1. Draw a diagonal line from corner to corner in both directions on the wrong side of the 2¾" background squares, using a pencil and ruler.

2. Layer a 2¾" background square on top of each of the 2¾" navy squares, right sides together. Stitch the squares together by sewing ¼" on each side of one of the diagonal lines as shown.

3. Cut the squares apart by cutting exactly on both drawn lines. Press the seam allowances toward the blue triangles. Notice that half of the triangle pairs will have the light triangle on the left and half will have the light triangle on the right.

 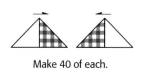

Cut apart.   Make 40 of each.

4. Sew identical pairs of triangles together, right sides together, to form quarter-square-triangle units. Make sure you don't have two navy triangles and two light triangles aligned; the colors should be opposite each other. The completed units will look like an hourglass or bow tie. Press the units and trim them to 2" square.

Make 40.

5. Using four identical quarter-square-triangle units, a matching 2" navy square, and four 2" background squares, lay out the block as shown. Take care to position the star points correctly. Sew the units together to form rows. Press the seam allowances toward the plain squares and then sew the rows together. Press. Repeat to complete 10 navy Ohio Star blocks.

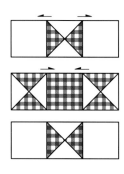 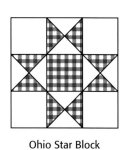

Ohio Star Block
Make 10.

6. Repeat steps 1 through 5, using the red squares and background pieces to make 10 red stars.

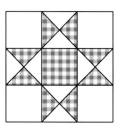

Make 10.

7. Make four corner Ohio Star blocks by reversing the values and using the navy squares.

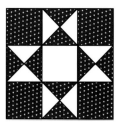

Make 4.

Assembling the Quilt

1. Referring to the assembly diagram below and the quilt photograph on page 28, arrange the Ohio Star blocks in five rows of four blocks each, alternating the navy and red stars.

2. Sew the blocks together into rows. Press the seams in opposite directions from one row to another.

   Note: Do not use the reverse color blocks for the quilt center. Reserve the light stars on navy background for the border corners.

3. Sew the rows together and press all seams in one direction.

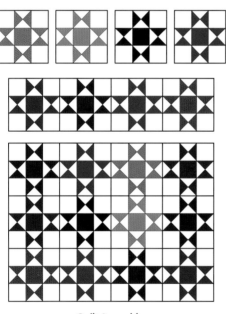

Quilt Assembly

Adding the Borders

1. Sew a 2"-wide background strip to either side of the 2"-wide red strips to make the borders. Press the seam allowances toward the red strips.

Make 4.

2. Measure the width and length of your quilt and trim two of the border strip sets to the same length as the quilt width (approximately 18½") and the remaining two strip sets to the same length as the quilt sides (approximately 22½").

3. Sew the shorter border strips to the top and bottom of the quilt and press the seams toward the borders.

4. Sew one of the light Ohio Star blocks to each end of the side border strips. Press the seam allowances toward the borders.

5. Sew the borders to the sides of the quilt and press the seam allowances toward the borders.

Quilt Plan

Finishing the Quilt

1. Trim the quilt backing so that it is approximately 3" larger than the quilt top.

2. Layer the quilt top, batting, and backing; baste the layers together.

3. Hand or machine quilt as desired. The quilt shown was quilted by hand with navy thread to outline the stars. A rope motif was also quilted in navy over the red and background borders.

4. Trim the excess batting and backing fabric ¼" from the outside edge.

5. Using the 2½"-wide navy print strips, make and attach the binding.

6. If desired, add a hanging sleeve and label your quilt.

Plaid Pineapple

Finished Quilt Size: 45½" x 57½" ◆ Finished Block Size: 12" x 12"

The Pineapple block is a variation of the ever-popular Log Cabin block. It's a fascinating block that looks difficult to make but is quite easy to do, especially when the blocks are large, as in this quilt, and foundation pieced. Your friends will think you are so clever when they see this intricate-looking quilt hanging on your wall. This quilt was made by my mother-in-law, Charlene Kimball.

MATERIALS

Yardages are based on 42"-wide fabrics.

◆ ½ yard *each* of 7 or 8 tartan plaids for blocks and pieced border

◆ 3 yards of navy blue print for blocks, outer border, and binding

◆ 2½ yards of red print for blocks and inner border

◆ 3 yards of backing fabric

◆ 50" x 62" piece of batting

◆ Paper for foundation piecing, large enough to accommodate 12" blocks

CUTTING

From *each* tartan plaid, cut:

2 strips, 1½" x 42", for pieced border

1½" wide *bias* strips, for pineapples, enough to equal 50" in length

From the red print, cut:

6 strips, 1½" x 42", for inner border, pieced border, and block centers

22 strips, 1½" x 42", for pineapples

From the navy print, cut:

5 strips, 2¼" x 42", for outer border

23 strips, 1½" x 42", for centers and pineapples

6 binding strips, 2½" x 42"

Making the Blocks

The blocks in this quilt are foundation pieced. You'll need to make 12 full-size copies of the foundation pattern, which is split into quadrants on pages 40–43. You can trace or photocopy the patterns and tape the four sections together to make a full-size pattern. Then trace, needle-punch, or photocopy the full-size pattern to make the necessary 12 copies. For more on making foundations and doing foundation piecing, see page 68.

Color Coding the Foundations

The Pineapple block has many pieces, so you may find it easier to stitch correctly and avoid mistakes if you color code the foundations. Simply indicate where the red, blue, and plaid pieces go by writing an *R* for red, *B* for blue, and *P* for plaid in each section with a colored pencil. It may take a little time to do this, but it's faster than trying to rip out a seam when you sew the wrong-color strip to the paper.

1. For the center four-patch units of the block, sew together a 1½"-wide red and a 1½"-wide navy strip. Press the seam allowance toward the navy strip. Crosscut the strip set into 1½"-wide segments. Cut 24.

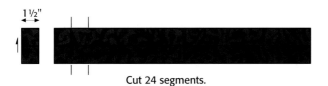

1½"

Cut 24 segments.

2. Sew the segments together in pairs, alternating the colors to make 12 four-patch units for the block centers. Press the seam allowances to one side.

Make 12.

3. Place a four-patch unit, right side up, on the wrong (unprinted) side of the pineapple foundation paper. Pin into position.

4. Holding the paper up to a light source with the printed side of the foundation facing you, position the first 1½"-wide plaid bias strip across the seam allowance of the center four-patch unit, right sides together. The bias strip should extend beyond the width of the four-patch center so that when it is sewn and turned back it will completely cover section 1 on the foundation and have enough extra for a seam allowance. Stitch on the printed side of the foundation paper. (If you are having difficulty seeing the seam line, fold the foundation paper

on the seam line.) Then flip the new strip into position, checking to see that it covers section 1.

fabric is used for all four sections in a single round.

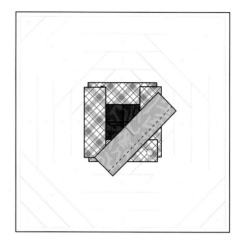

5. Carefully trim any excess fabric from the seam allowance and press the plaid strip in place; pin it to hold it in position.

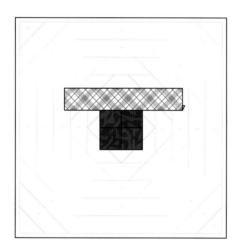

6. Continue to add strips in the same manner, following in the numerical sequence on the printed pattern. Pay close attention to the fabric placement, using plaid strips where indicated and red and blue strips in opposite corners. Note that, in the quilt shown, a different plaid fabric is used in each round, but the same plaid

Pineapple Block
Make 12.

7. Because the plaid strips are cut on the bias, it's a good idea to leave the paper foundations in place until the blocks are stitched together. The paper will add stability until the seams secure the edges and prevent stretching. However, if you prefer, you can remove the paper from the outer seam allowance area only. This will allow a tighter stitch in the seams joining the blocks, which will also add to the stability of bias pieces sewn together.

Assembling the Quilt

1. Referring to the assembly diagram below and the quilt photograph on page 33, arrange the Pineapple blocks in four rows of three blocks each. Make sure that the blocks are rotated so that the red corners and blue corners adjoin to form the overall design as shown.

2. Sew the blocks together into rows. Press the seams in opposite directions from one row to another.

3. Sew the rows together and press all seams in one direction.

Quilt Assembly

Adding the Borders

1. Measure the width of your quilt top, which should be 36½" wide. Trim two of the red 1½"-wide inner-border strips to this measurement and sew them to the top and bottom of the quilt. Press the seams toward the borders.

2. Measure the length of the quilt, which should be 50½". Sew the remaining three red inner-border strips together end to end, and from the long strip, cut two border strips the same length as the length of the quilt. Sew the strips to the sides of the quilt and press the seams toward the borders.

3. For the pieced border, sew leftover plaid bias strips together along their long edges. The strips won't all be the same length, but try to line them up as best as possible at one end in order to waste the least amount of fabric. Sew the strips together in manageable-width sets, about 12 to 18 strips per group. Press all the seams in one direction, taking care not to stretch the fabrics, since they are cut on the bias.

4. From the strip sets, cut 2¼"-wide segments. Sew these segments together end to end to make two borders at least 39" long and two borders at least 55" long. Trim all four border strips to 2¼" wide.

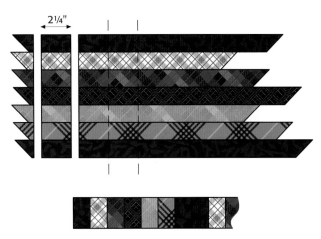

Make 4 borders.

5. Measure the width of your quilt and trim the two shorter border strips to this measurement, which should be approximately 38½". Note that you may need to trim the segments on the end of the border so they are not quite as wide as the other segments; however, make sure you don't trim either of them narrower than ¾", to allow for a seam allowance on each end. Sew these borders to the top and bottom of your quilt. Press the seams toward the red borders.

Foundation-Pieced Borders

If you are more comfortable with foundation piecing the borders because the plaid strips are cut on the bias, you can easily use this method. Simply draw out the width and length of the border needed on a piece of paper such as newsprint, freezer paper, or baking parchment (paper that will be long enough to accommodate your border length). Then stitch your pre-cut strips together on top of the paper, which will act as a stabilizer. Trim the excess fabric from each long side of the border strip and sew the strips to your quilt. Remove the paper after all piecing is complete.

6. Measure the length of your quilt and trim the two longer, pieced border strips to this measurement, which should be approximately 54". Sew these border strips to the sides of the quilt and press the seam allowances toward the red borders.

7. Measure the width of your quilt again, and trim two of the 2¼"-wide navy outer-border strips to this measurement, which should be 42".

   Note: If your fabric is narrower than 42" once the selvages are removed, then you will need to add a short piece of another 2¼"-wide navy strip to make the borders long enough.

   Sew the navy borders to the top and bottom of the quilt and press the seam allowances toward the navy borders.

8. Sew the three remaining 2¼"-wide navy strips together end to end. From this long strip, cut two side borders the same length as your quilt, which should be approximately 57½". Sew the borders to the sides of the quilt and press the seam allowances toward the navy borders.

Quilt Plan

Finishing the Quilt

1. Piece the quilt backing so that it is approximately 6" larger than the quilt top.

2. Layer the quilt top, batting, and backing; baste the layers together.

3. Hand or machine quilt as desired. The quilt shown was quilted by hand in the ditch of each round of pineapple pieces. The borders were simply quilted in the ditch along the long seams, although you could also quilt between each individual plaid segment if you so desire.

4. Trim the excess batting and backing fabric ¼" from the outside edge.

5. Using the 2½"-wide navy print strips, make and attach the binding.

6. If desired, add a hanging sleeve and label your quilt.

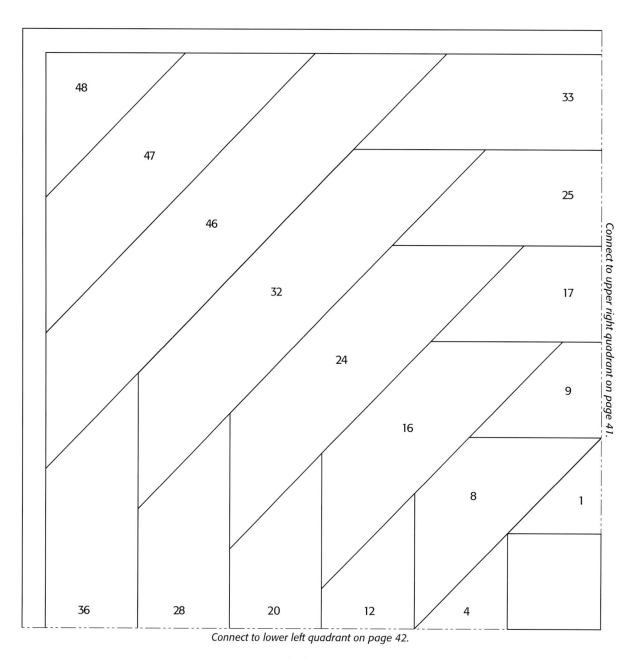

Connect to upper right quadrant on page 41.

Connect to lower left quadrant on page 42.

Foundation Pattern
Upper Left Quadrant

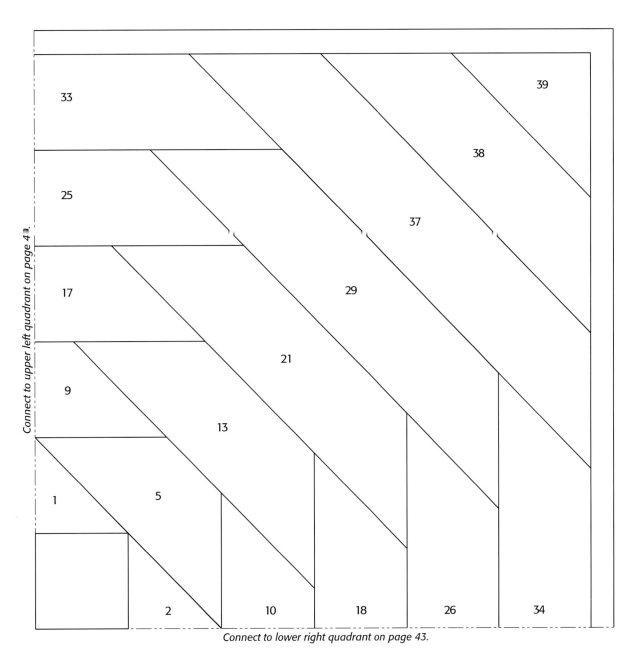

Foundation Pattern
Upper Right Quadrant

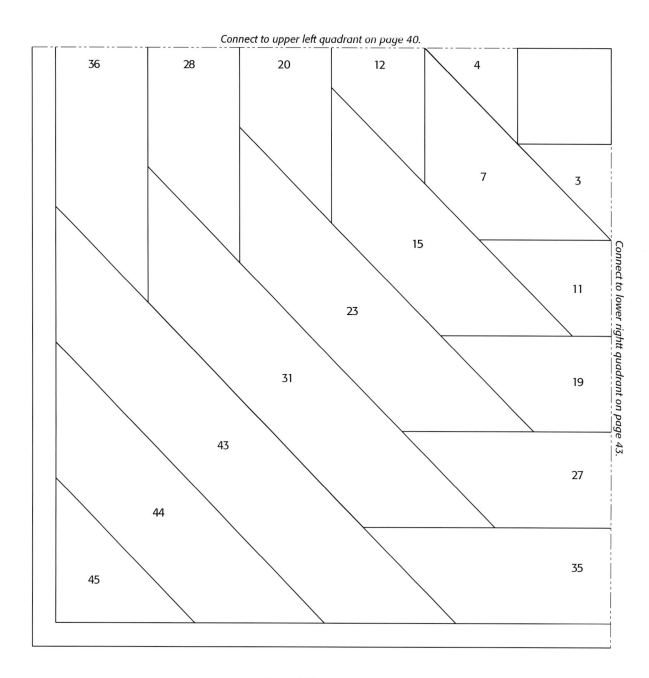

Connect to upper left quadrant on page 40.

Connect to lower right quadrant on page 43.

Foundation Pattern
Lower Left Quadrant

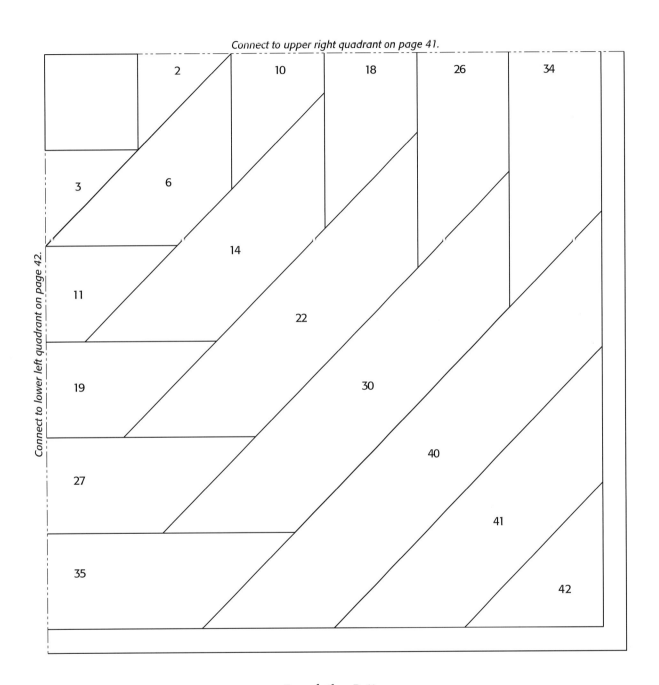

Connect to upper right quadrant on page 41.

Connect to lower left quadrant on page 42.

2
10
18
26
34

3
6

14

11

22

19

30

40

27

41

35

42

Foundation Pattern
Lower Right Quadrant

Caramel Apples

Finished Quilt Size: 88" x 96" ◆ Finished Block Size: 8½" x 8½"

Autumn is such a nice time of year, with leaves turning colors, a cool snap in the air, and seasonal treats like mulled cider, gingersnaps, and caramel apples to enjoy. You can bring this season into your home year-round with the rich, warm tones of this easy-to-make quilt. Using a mix of plaids and prints adds texture to the quilt design, so don't be afraid to use a wide assortment of plaid, striped, and printed fabrics. I only have one word of caution: this project may give you a caramel-apple craving!

MATERIALS

Yardages are based on 42"-wide fabrics.

◆ 3 yards of caramel print for borders

◆ 2½ yards of assorted dark red prints for blocks and pieced borders

◆ 2 yards of dark green print for outer border and binding

◆ 1½ yards of assorted light and medium golds and caramel prints for blocks

◆ 1½ yards of assorted light to medium red prints and plaids for triangles

◆ ¾ yard of assorted dark green prints and plaids for triangles

◆ 1 yard of assorted light to medium green prints and plaids for triangles

◆ ⅝ yard of dark red print for inner border

◆ 6 yards of backing fabric

◆ 94" x 102" piece of batting

CUTTING

From the assorted dark red prints, cut:

23 strips, 2" x 42"; crosscut strips into 452 squares, 2" x 2"

6 strips, 3½" x 42"; crosscut strips into 72 squares, 3½" x 3½"

From the assorted gold and caramel fabrics, cut:

27 strips, 2" x 42"; crosscut strips into 288 rectangles, 2" x 3½"

From the assorted dark green fabrics, cut:

32 squares, 5½"x 5½"; cut squares once diagonally to yield 64 triangles

From the assorted light and medium green fabrics, cut:

40 squares, 5½" x 5½"; cut squares once diagonally to yield 80 triangles

From the assorted light and medium red fabrics, cut:

72 squares, 5½" x 5½"; cut squares once diagonally to yield 144 triangles

From the dark red print for inner border, cut:

8 border strips, 2" x 42"

From the caramel print, cut:

9 border strips, 6" x 42"

11 strips, 2½" x 42"; crosscut strips into 172 squares, 2½" x 2½". Cut each square once diagonally to yield 328 A triangles for pieced border.

4 squares, 2¾" x 2¾"; cut squares twice diagonally to yield 16 B triangles for pieced border corners

From the dark green print, cut:

10 border strips, 2" x 42"

2¾"-wide bias strips, enough to yield 370" of binding

Making the Blocks

1. Sew a gold or caramel 2" x 3½" rectangle to opposite sides of the 3½" red squares. Make 72. Press the seam allowances toward the red fabric.

Make 72.

2. Sew a 2" red square to each end of the remaining gold and caramel rectangles. Press the seam allowances toward the red fabric.

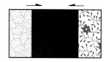

Make 144.

3. Sew the units from step 2 to the top and bottom of the units from step 1. Press. Make 72 units.

Make 72.

4. Keep the larger triangles separated into three main color groupings: dark green, light and medium green, and light and medium red. Sew triangles to opposite sides of a nine-patch unit, then sew two more triangles to the remaining two sides of the unit. Press all seams toward the triangles. The triangles on each block do not need to be from the same fabric, but they should be from the same color group. Make 16 with dark green triangles, 20 with light and medium green triangles, and 36 with light and medium red triangles.

Make 16.

Make 20.

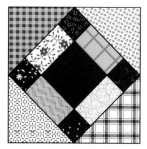

Make 36.

5. Trim the completed blocks to 9" x 9", making sure to trim them evenly from each side so that the nine-patch design is centered in the block.

Assembling the Quilt

1. Referring to the assembly diagram below and the quilt photograph on page 44, arrange the blocks in two different rows.

   Row A: Alternate red blocks with light and medium green blocks, with eight blocks per row. Make five of row A.

   Row B: Alternate dark green blocks with red blocks, with eight blocks per row. Make four of row B.

2. Sew the blocks together in rows, pressing the seams in opposite directions from one row to another.

3. Sew the rows together and press all seams in one direction.

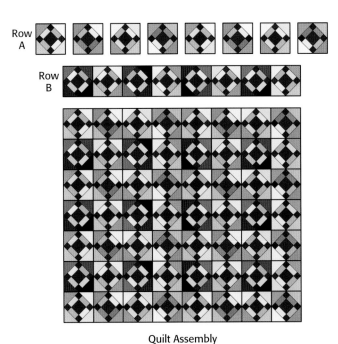

Quilt Assembly

Adding the Borders

1. Sew the 2"-wide dark red strips together in pairs to make four long inner border strips. Measure the width of the quilt and trim two of the red border strips to this measurement, which should be approximately 68". Sew them to the top and bottom of the quilt and press the seams toward the borders.

2. Measure the length of the quilt and trim the remaining two red border strips to this measurement, which should be approximately 80". Sew these border strips to the sides of the quilt. Press the seam allowances toward the borders.

3. Sew the 6"-wide caramel border strips together in pairs. Cut the remaining strip in half and sew one half to two of the longer strips.

4. Measure the width of the quilt, which should be approximately 71½", and trim the two shorter caramel border strips to this measurement. Sew the border strips to the top and bottom of the quilt and press the seams toward the caramel borders.

5. Measure the length of the quilt, which should be approximately 91½", and trim the two longer caramel border strips to this length. Sew the border strips to the sides of the quilt and press the seams toward the caramel borders.

6. For the pieced border, sew an A triangle to each side of 156 of the remaining 2" red squares. Press the seam allowances toward the squares.

Make 156.

7. Sew a B triangle to adjacent sides of the remaining eight 2" red squares. Then sew an A triangle to one side as shown to form the end units for the pieced borders.

Make 8.

8. Sew the triangle-and-square units together to make two strips of 37 units each. Add an end unit to each end of the strips, for a total of 39 red squares per strip. Press all seams in one direction, and then sew the strips to the top and bottom of quilt. Press the seam allowances toward the caramel border.

9. Sew the remaining triangle-and-square units together to make two strips of 41 units each. Add an end unit to the ends of each strip for a total of 43 squares per strip. Press all seams in one direction, and then sew the strips to the sides of the quilt. Press the seam allowances toward the caramel border.

10. Sew five of the dark green 2"-wide outer-border strips together end to end. Repeat with the remaining five strips. Measure the width of the quilt, which should be approximately 85¾". From one of the long border strips, cut two border strips to this measurement. Sew these border strips to the top and bottom of the quilt. Press the seam allowances toward the green borders.

11. Measure the length of the quilt, which should be approximately 98¼". From the long green border strip, cut two border strips to this length. Sew the border strips to the sides of the quilt and press the seam allowances toward the green borders.

Finishing the Quilt

1. Piece the quilt backing so that it is approximately 6" larger than the quilt top.

2. Layer the quilt top, batting, and backing; baste the layers together.

3. Hand or machine quilt as desired. The quilt shown was machine quilted by Cheryl Miller with apple-slice motifs in the blocks and a leaf-and-vine design in the wide caramel border.

4. Trim the excess batting and backing fabric ¼" from the outside edge.

5. Using the 2½"-wide dark green strips, make and attach the binding.

6. If desired, add a label to your quilt.

Quilt Plan

Cross Your Heart

Finished Quilt Size: 29½" x 29½" ◆ Finished Block Size: 6" x 6"

This little gem is made with madras plaids, which are such fun to work with for both patchwork and appliqué. Because the scale of the plaids tends to be larger than with other types of plaids, the color of your pieces can vary greatly from one cut piece to another. Depending on which part of the fabric you cut your appliqué pieces from, you can change the whole look of the design even though they're all cut from the same piece of fabric. My advice is to just enjoy the possibilities! No matter how you mix up the plaids, they will still coordinate. This quilt was designed by Debbie Bacon and made by Charlene Kimball.

MATERIALS

Yardages are based on 42"-wide fabrics.

- 1 yard of navy blue print for outer border and binding

- 1 yard of white solid for background

- ¼ yard *each* of 4 different madras plaids for baskets and appliqué

- ¼ yard of red solid for inner border and appliqué

- ¼ yard of light blue print for middle border

- ⅛ yard of dark green solid for baskets and stems

- 1 yard of backing fabric

- 34" x 34" piece of batting

- Red, green, navy, and white embroidery floss

CUTTING

From the madras plaids, cut:

8 squares, 2⅜" x 2⅜"; cut squares once diagonally to yield 16 triangles

4 squares, 3⅞" x 3⅞"; cut squares once diagonally to yield 8 triangles

From the white solid background fabric, cut:

2 squares, 12⅞" x 12⅞"; cut squares once diagonally to yield 4 corner triangles

8 squares, 2⅜" x 2⅜"; cut squares once diagonally to yield 16 triangles

4 squares, 2" x 2"

8 rectangles, 2" x 3½"

2 squares, 3⅞" x 3⅞"; cut squares once diagonally to yield 4 triangles

From the dark green solid, cut:

4 squares, 2⅜" x 2⅜"; cut squares once diagonally to yield 8 triangles

From the red solid, cut:

2 border strips, 1¼" x 42"

From the light blue print, cut:

4 border strips, 1¾" x 42"

From the navy print, cut:

4 border strips, 4½" x 42"

3 binding strips, 2½" x 42"

Making the Blocks

1. With right sides together, sew the 3⅞" madras triangles together to make four triangle squares. Mix and match the colors as desired. Press the seam allowances toward the darker fabric.

Make 4.

2. Sew the 2⅜" white triangles to the 2⅜" madras triangles to make 16 triangle squares. Press the seams toward the madras triangles.

Make 16.

3. Sew the 2" triangle squares together in pairs, making sure half the pairs point to the left and half point to the right as shown.

Make 4.   Make 4.

4. Using the large triangle squares, the 2" white squares, and the pairs of small triangle squares, lay out the pieces as shown. Stitch the pieces together in rows, and then stitch the rows together. Press.

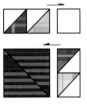

Make 4.

5. Sew the dark green triangles to the 2" x 3½" white rectangles. Make four units with the triangle on the right and four with the triangle on the left as shown. Sew these units to either side of the units from step 4. Press the seam allowances toward the rectangles.

Make 4 of each.

6. Sew a 3⅞" white triangle to the bottom of each block. Press and then square up the block, trimming off any dog ears from the triangles.

Cake Stand Block
Make 4.

Assembling the Quilt

1. Sew the four Cake Stand blocks together to form a diamond-shaped center medallion.

2. With right sides together and centers matching, sew the large white triangles to each corner of the medallion. These triangles are larger than needed. After pressing the seam allowances, trim the excess fabric to square up the quilt. Be sure not to trim off the ¼" seam allowance.

3. Cut the two red inner-border strips in half so you have two pieces, each about 20" long. Measure the length and width of your quilt top, which should be approximately 17" x 17". Then mark the center of each border strip and measure from the center to each end of the border to mark the distance equal to one-half the length of the quilt.

4. Sew a red border strip to each side of the quilt, starting and stopping ¼" from the end of the quilt and the border markings. Then miter the border corners, referring to "Mitered Borders" on page 74. Press the border seams toward the red fabric and press the mitered corner seams open or to one side.

5. Measure the length and width of your quilt. It should now be approximately 19" x 19". Trim each of the light blue border strips to about 25", or at least 5" longer that the width of your quilt. Attach the light blue borders in the same manner as for the red inner borders and miter the corners. Press the seams toward the light blue borders.

6. For the outer border, trim the navy print strips to at least 32". Attach the navy borders in the same manner as for the other borders and miter the corners. Press the seams toward the navy borders.

Appliqué

The quilt shown was appliquéd by hand, but if you prefer, you can use fusible appliqué. The instructions below are for hand appliqué, including reversible appliqué used for the hearts in the center of the tulips.

1. Mark the placement for appliqué on each large white corner of the quilt interior by lightly tracing the appliqué pattern on page 55. Make templates from the pattern for your favorite appliqué method, using freezer paper, template plastic, or fusible web.

2. From the dark green solid fabric, cut a ¾"-wide bias strip for the stems. Fold the bias strip in half lengthwise, wrong sides together. Sew ¼" from the raw edges, and then trim the seam allowance to ⅛".

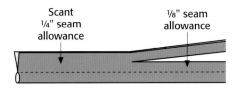

Scant ¼" seam allowance

⅛" seam allowance

3. Place the raw edges of the folded bias ⅛" inside the marked line on the background triangle. Sew in place along the stitched seam line, sewing by hand with a small running stitch or by machine. Finger-press the bias stem over the stitched line and sew the folded edge in place with a blind stitch.

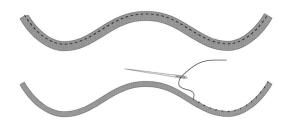

4. For each of the four tulips, mark the tulip shape and the interior heart shape on the right side of a 3" x 4" scrap of plaid fabric. The heart shape will be cut away to reveal an underneath layer of fabric.

Mark heart design.

5. Pin a piece of red solid fabric underneath the marked heart on each tulip appliqué. Make sure the fabric is large enough to extend beyond the drawn lines by at least ¼". Baste the fabrics together and remove the pins.

6. Using sharp embroidery scissors, trim the top fabric inside of the drawn line, leaving about ⅛" of plaid fabric inside of the drawn heart. Using the needle to help turn the top fabric under, turn under the heart shape along the marked line, clipping curves and points as you go. Hand stitch the folded edges in place.

7. After the heart shape has been completely stitched, press the appliqué and trim the excess red fabric from the back of the quilt.

8. Trim around the marked line for the tulip shape, leaving a ¼" seam allowance, and appliqué it to the background fabric. Repeat for all four tulips.

9. Prepare the remaining appliqués and stitch them in place: 8 plaid hearts, 4 red hearts, 16 red berries, 12 plaid flourishes. Note that the red hearts were also reverse appliquéd in the quilt shown.

10. Prepare four additional red hearts and appliqué them in the corner of each light blue border.

11. Add the embroidery details to the appliqué, using two strands of embroidery floss. The quilt shown has white French knots stitched around the heart inside the tulip, navy French knots stitched around the larger red heart, green stems stitched to the berries, and red flourishes and French knots stitched above the plaid hearts. (See "Stitch Dictionary" on page 79.)

Quilt Plan

Finishing the Quilt

1. Trim the quilt backing so that it is approximately 6" larger than the quilt top.

2. Layer the quilt top, batting, and backing; baste the layers together.

3. Hand or machine quilt as desired. The quilt shown was hand quilted. The basket blocks were quilted in the ditch, while the larger areas of white background fabric were quilted in a crosshatch pattern. The navy border was also quilted with cross-hatching.

4. Trim the excess batting and backing fabric ¼" from the outside edge.

5. Using the 2½"-wide navy print strips, make and attach the binding.

6. If desired, add a hanging sleeve and label your quilt.

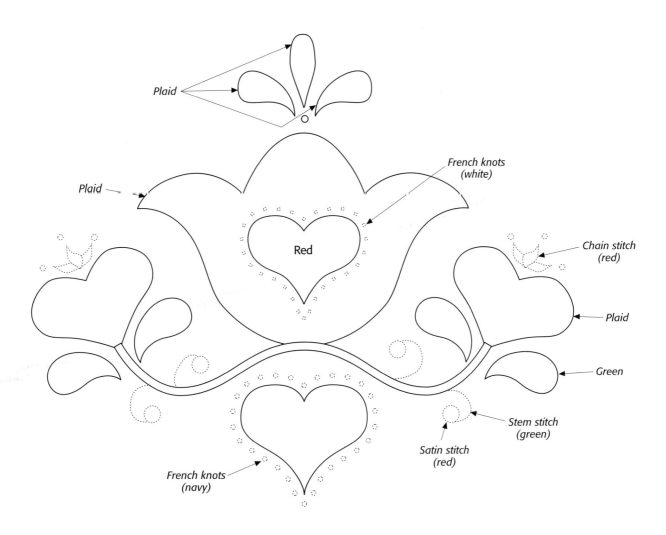

Plaid

Plaid

French knots
(white)

Red

Chain stitch
(red)

Plaid

Green

Stem stitch
(green)

Satin stitch
(red)

French knots
(navy)

Appliqué Patterns and Placement Guide

Patterns do not include seam allowances.
Add ¼" seam allowances for hand appliqué.
Hearts are reverse appliquéd.

Cherry Squares

Finished Quilt Size: 41½" x 41½" ◆ Finished Block Size: 7" x 7"

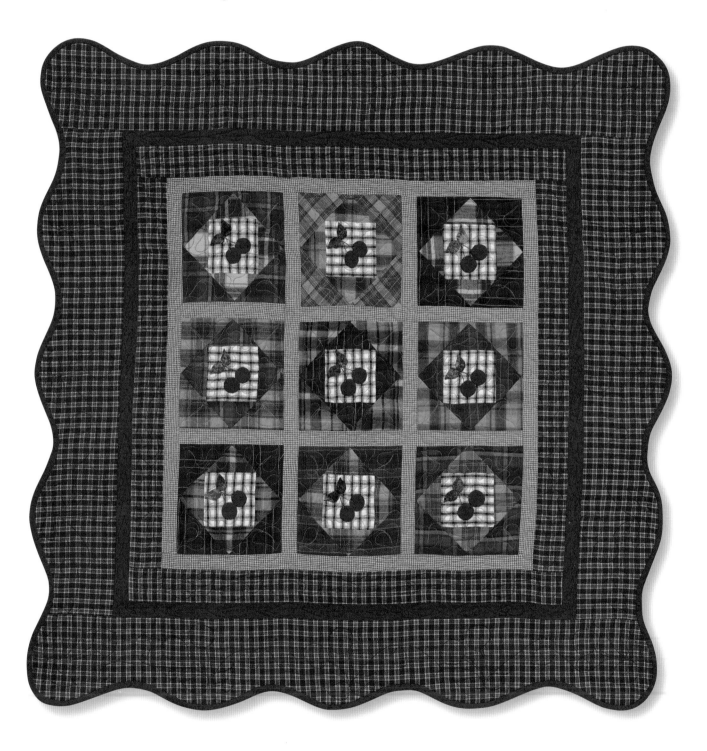

Every year my grandmother would pick cherries from her cherry tree and "put them up" for the winter. But in August, she would open a jar of those cherries and make me the best cherry cobbler for my birthday. This quilt is dedicated to her and all the great treats she brought into our lives.

MATERIALS

Yardages are based on 42"-wide fabrics.

◆ ¼ yard *each* of 9 assorted bright plaids for blocks

◆ 1¼ yards of red plaid for borders

◆ l yard of red print for cherries, border, and bias binding

◆ ¼ yard of light background plaid for block centers

◆ ¼ yard of light green check for sashing

◆ ⅛ yard of green print for leaves

◆ 1¼ yards of backing fabric

◆ 48" x 48" piece of batting

◆ Green embroidery floss for stems

CUTTING

From the light background plaid, cut:

1 strip, 4" x 42"; crosscut strip into 9 squares, 4" x 4"

From *each* of the bright plaids, cut:

1 square, 4¾" x 4¾"; cut squares twice diagonally to yield 4 inside triangles (36 total)

2 squares, 4½" x 4½"; cut squares once diagonally to yield 4 outside triangles (36 total)

From the light green check, cut:

6 strips, 1½" x 42"

From the red plaid, cut on the *lengthwise* grain:

4 inner-border strips, 2½" x 45"

4 outer-border strips, 6" x 45"

From the red print, cut:

18 cherries

4 middle-border strips, 1½" x 42"

2½"-wide bias strips, enough to yield 174" for binding

From the green print, cut:

9 pairs of leaves

Making the Blocks

1. Using the patterns on page 61, prepare 18 cherries in the red print and 18 leaves in the green print for your favorite appliqué method. Hand or machine appliqué the cherries and leaves onto the 4" light plaid squares. Embroider the stems using the stem stitch (see "Stitch Dictionary" on page 79) and green floss. Press the blocks.

2. Sew a matching set of inside plaid triangles around each cherry square by sewing first the top and bottom triangles followed by the side triangles. Press the seams toward the triangles. Trim the blocks so they measure 5⅜" square.

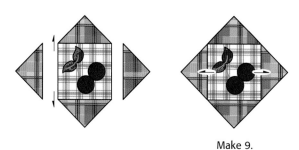

Make 9.

3. Sew a matching set of outside plaid triangles around each cherry square by sewing them to two opposite sides of the block and then to the remaining two sides. Press all seams toward the outside triangles. Square up each block so that it measures 7½" square.

Make 9.

Assembling the Quilt

1. From each 1½" x 42" green check strip, cut one short sashing strip, 1½" x 7½". Arrange the blocks and short sashing strips in three vertical rows. Sew the pieces together, pressing the seam allowances toward the sashing strips.

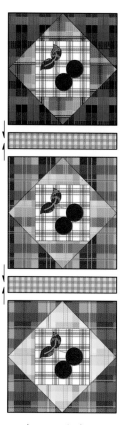

Make 3 vertical rows.

2. Measure the length of the block rows. They should be approximately 23½" long. (If they differ, use the average length.) Trim four of the long sashing strips to this length. Then, referring to the quilt assembly diagram, opposite,

and the quilt photograph on page 56, sew the three block rows and the four sashing strips together. Press the seams toward the sashing.

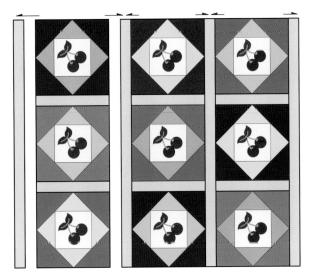

Quilt Assembly

3. Measure the width of your quilt top, which should be approximately 25½", and trim the remaining two sashing strips to this length. Sew them to the top and bottom of the quilt. Press the seam allowances toward the sashing.

Adding the Borders

1. Measure the length of your quilt and trim two of the 2½" x 45" red plaid border strips to this length, which should be approximately 25½". Sew the strips to the sides of the quilt and press the seams toward the borders. In the same manner, measure the width of the quilt and trim the remaining two 2½" x 45" red plaid strips to that length, which should be approximately 29½". Sew these border strips to the top and bottom of the quilt and press the seams toward the borders.

2. Measure the length of the quilt top, which should now be approximately 29½". Trim two of the red print border strips to this length. Sew them to the sides of the quilt and press the seams toward the red borders. Repeat for the red top and bottom borders. The length of the quilt should now be approximately 31½".

3. Measure the length of the quilt top as for the other borders and trim two of the 6" x 45" red plaid border strips to this length, which should be approximately 31½". Sew the border strips to the sides of the quilt. Measure for the top and bottom border strips, which should be approximately 42½" long. Sew these border strips to the top and bottom of the quilt. Press as for the other borders.

Quilt Plan

Finishing the Quilt

1. Piece the quilt backing so that it is approximately 6" larger than the quilt top.

2. Layer the quilt top, batting, and backing; baste the layers together.

3. Hand or machine quilt as desired, except for the outer border. The quilt shown was machine quilted by Mary Covey with meandering leaves. The outer border (quilted after the scalloped border is completed) was quilted with cherries and leaves.

4. Make a freezer-paper or plastic template of the scalloped border pattern on page 62 and of the scalloped corner pattern on page 63. Use these templates to mark the scalloped curves on your quilt borders. You will have three scallops per side, plus the scalloped corners. The dashed line on the pattern indicates where to match up the scallops.

   Lay the template (or press the freezer-paper template in place) on the border, aligning the long, straight edge with the seam line between the red plaid and red print borders. Mark the scallops with a chalk pencil or other visible marker. This will be the edge of the quilt and will be covered by binding, so it's not critical that the mark be removable.

5. Sew the 2½"-wide red bias strips together end to end to form one long strip of bias binding. Fold the strip in half lengthwise, wrong sides together, and press. Sew the binding to the quilt, matching the raw edges with the marked line. (The folded edge should face toward the center of the quilt.) Leave a 3" tail of binding for finishing the ends and stitch the binding in place, sewing ¼" from the raw edges of the binding. Gently ease in the fullness around the inside curves. Be careful not to pull the binding along the outer curves.

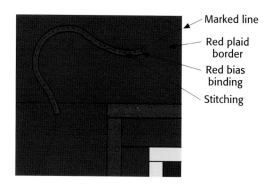

Marked line
Red plaid border
Red bias binding
Stitching

6. Trim the excess batting, backing, and quilt-top fabric, leaving a ¼" seam allowance to fill out the binding.

7. Finish quilting the border area and then finish the binding by folding it to the back of the quilt and stitching it in place.

8. If desired, add a hanging sleeve and label your quilt.

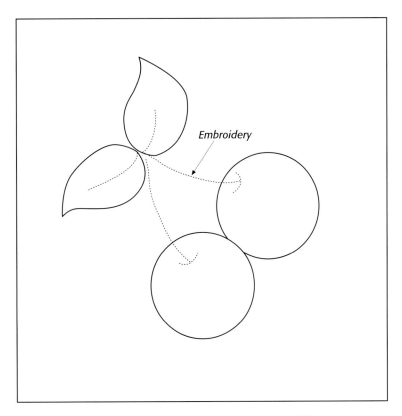

Embroidery

Appliqué Patterns and Placement Guide

Patterns do not include seam allowances.
Add ¼" seam allowances for hand appliqué.

Scalloped Border Pattern

Patterns do not include seam allowances.
Add ¼" seam allowances for hand appliqué.

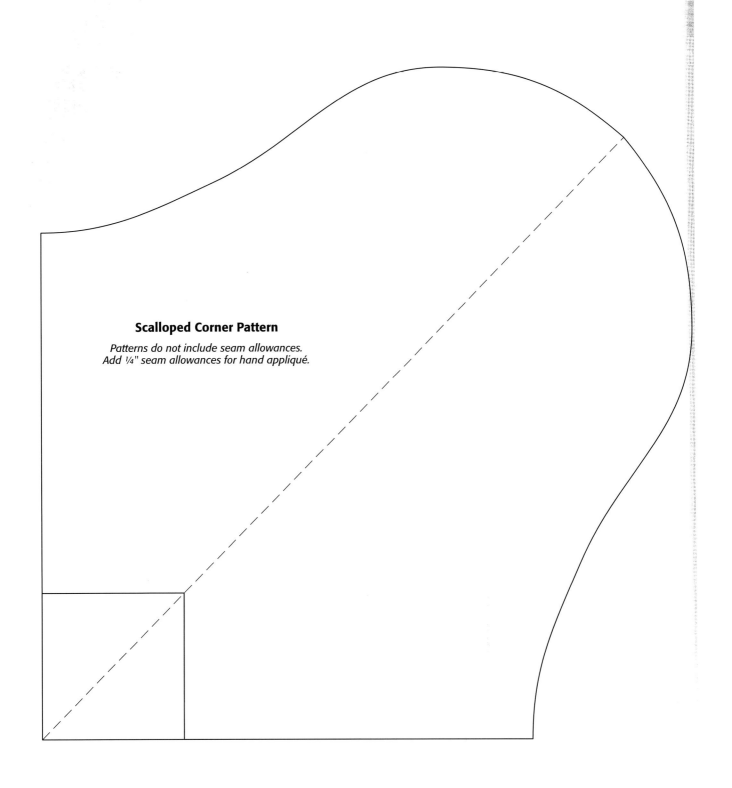

Scalloped Corner Pattern

Patterns do not include seam allowances.
Add ¼" seam allowances for hand appliqué.

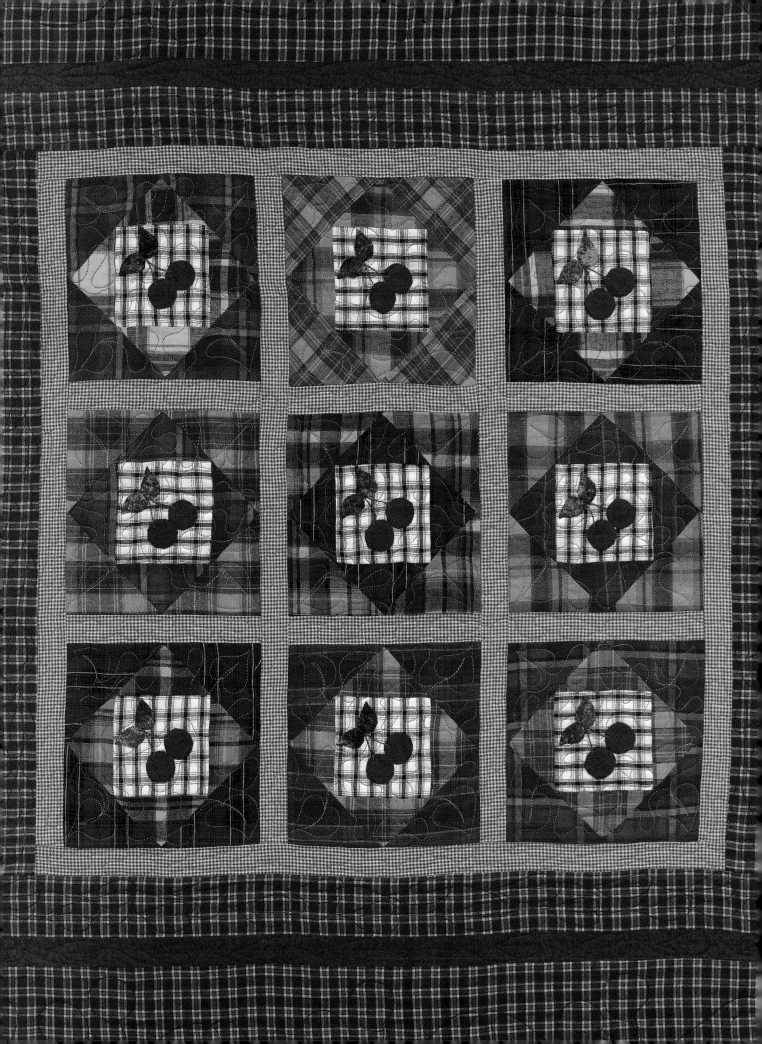

Quiltmaking Basics

Every quiltmaker has her favorite methods, and in this section I'll share mine with you. Whether you're looking for some inspiration to try a new technique or you just want to review the basics, I hope the information presented here will help you achieve success with your next project.

Fabrics

For most quilts, 100%-cotton fabrics are the best choice because they are stable for cutting and sewing and they're easy to care for. I recommend prewashing fabrics before using them in a quilt. When working with plaid fabrics, there are a few things to consider.

- A woven plaid is reversible, whereas a printed plaid is not. In addition, printed plaids are often not printed on the straight of grain. If you like the look of folk art and don't mind your plaid patches looking a little off-kilter, then printed plaids may work well for you. On the other hand, if you want all plaids to appear perfectly cut in your quilt, you may want to stick with woven plaids.

- Flannel plaids are popular and they can be used in some of the quilts. However, because of the bulk of the fabric, avoid designs that have many intersecting points, such as a star design. "Churn Dash" on page 23 or "Caramel Apples" on page 44 would be nice in flannel.

- Plaids, by their very nature, contain a lot of lines in the design. Unlike garment sewing, matching the lines in the plaids is not something you need to worry about. In fact, when the plaids are slightly mismatched, it makes for a very interesting quilt!

Notice how the dark lines in the red plaid do not match or align from one patch to the next.

Rotary Cutting

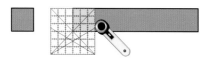

Instructions for quick-and-easy rotary cutting are provided wherever possible. All measurements include standard ¼"-wide seam allowances. If you are unfamiliar with rotary cutting, read the brief instructions below. For more detailed information, see *Shortcuts: A Concise Guide to Rotary Cutting* by Donna Lynn Thomas (Martingale & Company, 1999).

1. To cut squares, cut a strip in the required width. Trim the selvage ends of the strip. Align the left edge of the strip with the correct ruler markings. The sides of each square should have the same measurement as the width of the strip. Cut the strip into squares. Continue cutting squares until you have the number needed.

2. To make a half-square triangle, begin by cutting a square ⅞" larger than the desired finished size of the short side of the triangle. Then cut the square once diagonally, corner to corner. Each square yields two half-square triangles. The short sides of each triangle are on the straight grain of the fabric. When two different half-square triangles are sewn together to make a pieced square, the unit is called a triangle square or bias square.

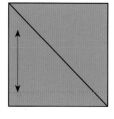

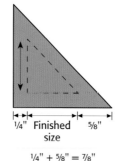

¼" + ⅝" = ⅞"

Triangles on a Roll

Some folks like to use a paper foundation to make triangle squares. With this technique, the fabrics are stitched to preprinted papers, so all the squares turn out accurately and are exactly the same size. If you like to do group swaps, as I've done for the blocks in "Shadow Plaid" on page 13 and "Churn Dash" on page 23, you might find that Triangles on a Roll grid paper is handy. If everyone in the group uses it, there's no worry that someone's triangle squares will turn out too large or too small. Everyone uses the same-size paper foundations and directions, which makes all the triangle squares a perfect fit in the end.

3. To make a quarter-square triangle, begin by cutting a square 1¼" larger than the desired finished size of the long edge of the triangle. Then cut the square twice diagonally, corner to corner. Each square yields four quarter-square triangles. The long side of each triangle is on the straight grain of the fabric.

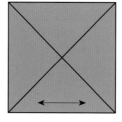

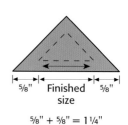

⅝" Finished size ⅝"

⅝" + ⅝" = 1¼"

MACHINE PIECING

The most important thing to remember about machine piecing is that you need to maintain a consistent ¼"-wide seam allowance. Otherwise, the quilt blocks will not be the desired finished size. If that happens, the size of everything else in the quilt is affected, including alternate blocks, sashings, and borders.

Take the time to establish an exact ¼"-wide seam guide on your machine. Some machines have a special quilting foot that measures exactly ¼" from the center needle position to the edge of the foot. This feature allows you to use the edge of the presser foot to guide the fabric for a perfect ¼"-wide seam allowance. If your machine doesn't have such a foot, create a seam guide by placing the edge of a piece of tape, moleskin, or a magnetic seam guide ¼" away from the needle.

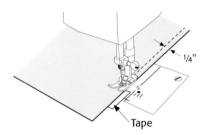

Tape

Chain Piecing

Chain piecing is an efficient system that saves time and thread. It's especially useful when you're making many identical units.

1. Sew the first pair of pieces from cut edge to cut edge, using 12 to 15 stitches per inch. At the end of the seam, stop sewing but do not cut the thread.

2. Feed the next pair of pieces under the presser foot, as close as possible to the first. Continue feeding pieces through the machine without cutting the threads in between the pairs.

3. When all the pieces are sewn, remove the chain from the machine and clip the threads between the pairs of sewn pieces.

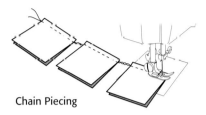

Chain Piecing

Quick Piecing Units

Triangle squares and quarter-square-triangle units are commonly used in quiltmaking. You can cut the individual pieces from a square, as described above in "Rotary Cutting," and sew them back together, mixing and matching the colors. Or, you can use these shortcut techniques that some quiltmakers just love.

Triangle Squares

1. Cut squares from two different fabrics. The squares should be at least ⅞" larger than you want your finished unit to be. If you add more than ⅞" to your cut size, it will give you a little extra to trim off to make perfectly sized triangle squares.

2. On the wrong side of the lighter-color square, draw a diagonal line from one corner to the opposite corner, or fold the square in half diagonally to mark the diagonal with a crease.

3. Layer the squares right sides together and stitch ¼" away from each side of the drawn line or crease.

4. Cut the squares apart on the marked line and press open the two resulting triangle squares.

Yields 2
triangle squares.

Quarter-Square Triangles

1. Cut squares from two different fabrics. For these units, you need to cut the squares at least 1¼" larger than you want your finished units to be.

2. As for "Triangle Squares" on page 67, mark the diagonal line from corner to corner and also mark the opposite diagonal.

3. Layer the squares right sides together and stitch ¼" away from each side of *one* of the diagonal lines.

4. Cut the triangles apart on *both* solid lines.

5. Sew the resulting pairs of triangles together so the adjoining triangles will be opposite colors.

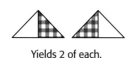

Yields 2 of each.   Yields 2 quarter-square units.

Pressing

The traditional rule in quiltmaking is to press seams to one side, toward the darker color wherever possible. First press the seams flat from the wrong side of the fabric; then press the seams in the desired direction from the right side. Press carefully to avoid distorting the shapes.

When joining two seamed units, plan ahead and press the seam allowances in opposite directions as shown. This reduces bulk and makes it easier to match the seam lines. The seam allowances will butt against each other where two seams meet, making it easier to sew units with perfectly matched seam intersections.

Opposing Seams

Foundation Piecing

Also referred to as *paper piecing,* this technique is a little more time-consuming than traditional patchwork, but the results are precise. Foundation piecing is perfect for projects like "Plaid Pineapple" on page 33, where you need to sew together many pieces with bias edges. Stitching the fabrics to a paper pattern stabilizes the patchwork.

You'll need a lightweight paper that's easy to see through for making foundations. Tracing paper and baking parchment make good foundations; besides allowing you to see through them, they're also easy to tear away when the blocks have been completed. Martingale & Company packages paper specifically for foundation piecing, which you can find at your local quilt shop. These papers can be used in computer laser printers as well as in photocopy machines.

Copying Foundations

Be careful about using photocopied foundation patterns. Depending on the copier used, they can be a little distorted. And sometimes the ink from the photocopier will transfer to your fabrics when you press them with an iron. If you use a copier, measure the pattern before using it to make sure it's accurate and also test to make sure the ink won't rub off onto your fabrics.

If you have problems with the copier, you can trace the pattern from your book to the foundation paper. Use a ruler to make sure all lines are straight and accurate. It can be time-consuming to trace multiple patterns, so another option is to make one tracing and then needle-punch multiple copies with your sewing machine. Place your original pattern on top of additional sheets of foundation paper. Then, with no thread in your machine, stitch over every line in the pattern. The design will be punched into all the layers.

1. Make one foundation for each block in your quilt.

2. Cut fabric strips that are wide enough to cover the entire area plus seam allowances. It's best to err on the side of too much fabric than to skimp on your strips here!

3. Hold the foundation paper printed side down/ wrong side facing up, and then center the fabric that is to cover the center of the block so that all seam lines are covered. Pin the fabric in place.

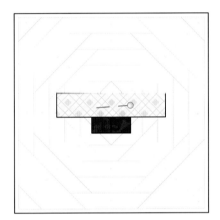

Pin.

4. With right sides together, place the next strip to be added on top of the center fabric, making sure the raw edges extend at least ¼" beyond the stitching line to account for a seam allowance. Turn the foundation over and sew on the line to attach the center piece and the next strip to the foundation paper.

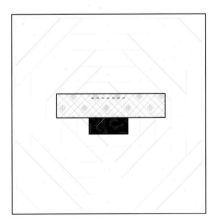

Sew.

5. Flip the new piece into its position to make sure it extends into the next seam allowance. Trim any excess fabric from the seam you just stitched, and then finger-press the piece open.

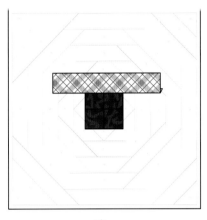

Flip.

6. Repeat the process, adding new pieces, trimming away excess fabric, and pressing open the pieces until all sections of the foundation paper are covered. You can trim excess fabric from the edges of the block, but be sure to maintain a ¼" seam allowance around the perimeter of the block.

7. Remove the paper by gently tearing the paper along the stitching lines. You can either remove the paper before or after sewing the blocks together.

Appliqué

Appliqué is the process of adding a piece of fabric on top of another piece of fabric. Appliqué shapes can be stitched in place by hand or machine or fused in place with fusible web. You can even cut away the top layer of fabric to reveal another fabric below. This method is called reverse appliqué. The various types of appliqué are explained in more detail on the following pages. Any of the techniques can be used to make the projects in this book.

Needle-Turn Appliqué

With this method, the appliqués are stitched in place by hand, and the tip of the needle is used to turn under the seam allowance as you go.

1. Make a plastic template for each shape in your appliqué design. Label each template with the name of the piece so you will know which is the right side.

2. Trace around the templates onto the right side of the appliqué fabric, allowing at least ½" between shapes. Then cut out the appliqués, cutting roughly ¼" outside of the drawn lines.

3. Position the appliqué pieces on the background fabric, right side up. Pin or baste them in place.

4. Use the tip of your needle to turn under the edge of the appliqué for a distance of only about ½". Use your thumb or finger to crease the edge where the seam is turned under and to hold it in place as you stitch. You will need to clip curves and points to ensure that the seam allowance turns under smoothly.

5. Using a blind stitch, sew the appliqué shape in place.

Needle-Turn Appliqué

6. If your appliqué design has multiple pieces layered over one another, begin stitching the bottom piece first and build toward the foreground. You do not need to turn under any edges that will be covered by other appliqué shapes.

Freezer-Paper Appliqué

Freezer paper, which is sold in grocery stores in the same aisle as plastic wrap and aluminum foil, is quite handy for appliqué templates. It's plastic-coated on one side, so you can iron the shapes to your fabric and they will adhere as the plastic is warmed. When you're through appliquéing, the freezer-paper shapes peel off easily.

Freezer paper on top. With this method, you are essentially doing needle-turn appliqué. Instead of tracing around a plastic template onto your appliqué fabric to mark the seam lines, you mark the lines on the freezer paper.

1. Cut out the freezer-paper shapes exactly on the drawn line, press them onto the right side of your appliqué fabrics, and cut out the shapes, leaving about a ¼" seam allowance beyond the freezer paper.

2. Use the blind stitch as for regular needle-turn appliqué to sew the shape in place. With this method, you'll have the firm edge of the freezer paper as your turn-under guide.

3. Stitch completely around the shape and then pull off the freezer paper.

Freezer-Paper Template
on Appliqué

Freezer paper underneath. The other way to use freezer paper for appliqué is to use it as a foundation beneath your appliqué fabric.

1. Make the paper templates as before, lay the freezer-paper template (paper side toward the fabric) on the wrong side of fabric, and trace around the shape with a chalk pencil.

2. Cut out the shape, leaving a ¼" seam allowance around the outside of the chalk line.

3. Lay the template back on the wrong side of the fabric shape, paper side down. Gently fold the seam allowance onto the shiny side of the paper. Press the seam allowance with a warm iron to hold it in place. You will need to clip curves and points to get the seam allowance to fold neatly into place.

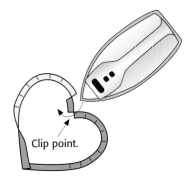

Clip point.

4. Pin the appliqué to the background fabric and use a blind stitch to secure it.

5. To remove the freezer paper, carefully cut a slit in the background fabric only beneath the appliqué shape. Pull out the freezer paper with your fingers or a pair of tweezers. If desired, you can trim away the background fabric from behind the appliqué, but be sure to leave a ¼" seam allowance.

Back of appliqué block

REVERSE APPLIQUÉ

In reverse appliqué, the appliqué shape is cut away from the top layer of fabric to reveal the fabric below. This technique is particularly helpful for shapes with convex curves, such as circles or hearts. You'll find that it is quite easy to turn the seam allowances under when you reverse appliqué these shapes as compared to traditional hand appliqué.

1. Draw the design on the right side of the top fabric.

2. Pin the second fabric underneath the top fabric, with its right side up. Baste the two fabrics together, outside of the drawn design.

3. Using sharp embroidery scissors, carefully cut away the design area from the top fabric only. Cut about ⅛" inside the drawn line to leave a seam allowance.

4. Appliqué the top fabric to the bottom fabric along the drawn line, using the tip of the needle to help turn the seam allowance as you go. Clip all curves and corners as you approach them.

5. Press the appliqué and trim the excess fabric from the wrong side, leaving about a ¼" seam allowance.

Bias Tubes

Narrow strips cut on the bias and then stitched into tubes are an easy way to make stems for floral appliqué. A set of bias bars is handy to have on hand for this technique. Bias bars are strips of metal or nylon and are usually packaged in sets of varying widths so that you can make your bias stems, or basket handles as wide or as narrow as you'd like.

1. The finished size of your tube will determine how wide you need to cut your bias strips:

   ¼" tube: cut a 1"-wide bias strip

   ⅜" tube: cut a 1¼"-wide bias strip

   ½" tube: cut a 1½"-wide bias strip

2. Fold the strip in half lengthwise, *wrong* sides together. Press the fold.

3. Stitch the raw edges of the bias strip together, stitching as far away from the fold as the finished width of your bias tube. For instance, for a ¼" bias tube, stitch ¼" away from the fold; for a ⅜" bias tube, sew ⅜" from the fold; and for a ½" tube, sew ½" away from the fold. For all sizes, trim the excess fabric, leaving approximately ⅛" for a seam allowance.

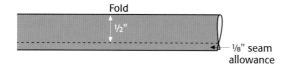

4. Insert the appropriate-size bias bar into the bias tube. Then rotate the tube so that the seam allowance is centered under one side of the bar. Press with steam. If your bias tube is longer than the bar, press at one end, slide the bar along into the tube, and press the next section. Continue scooting the bar along the length of the tube until the entire bias tube is pressed. Your bias tube is now ready to appliqué in place.

Fusible Appliqué

Fusible appliqué is a quick and easy way to create beautiful appliqué projects. I recommend that you read the instructions that come with your fusible web before adhering it to your fabric. Lightweight fusible web is suitable for stitching through; heavy-duty fusible web is not recommended for stitching through with a machine. Different brands may also recommend different pressing times; pressing too long may result in appliqués that don't stick well.

1. Trace or draw the appliqué shape onto the paper-backing side of the fusible web using a permanent marker or pencil. If your appliqué pattern is directional, you will need to reverse the direction before transferring it to your fusible web; otherwise, the pattern will be adhered to the wrong side of your fabric. Dotted lines on the pattern indicate where some pieces may fit under other pieces.

2. Cut out each shape, leaving about ¼" outside of the outline.

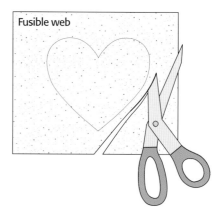

Trimming Large Shapes

If the appliqué pieces are very large, also trim the inside of the fusible web up to ¼" from the seam allowance. This will make the finished appliqués less stiff, and it will be easier to layer other pieces on top.

3. Fuse each piece of fusible web onto the wrong side of your selected appliqué fabrics.

4. Cut out the shapes exactly on the marked outlines.

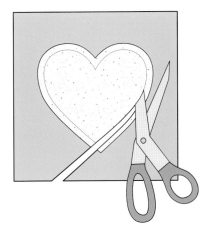

5. Remove the paper backing from the fusible web, arrange the appliqué pieces onto the background fabric, and press them in place with your iron.

6. Machine or hand appliqué around each piece, using either a satin stitch or the blanket stitch and referring to "Stitch Dictionary" on page 79.

Quilt Settings

Quilt blocks can be sewn together in horizontal rows, called a straight set, or in diagonal rows, called a diagonal or on-point set.

Straight Set

1. Lay out all the quilt blocks. Check to make sure all the blocks are the same size and correct any that may not match. You may need to trim them up a bit or adjust a seam allowance here or there.

2. With right sides together, sew the blocks together into rows. Press the seams in one direction in one row and the opposite direction in the next row.

3. With right sides together, sew the rows together. For a quilt top that lies flat, press the seams all in one direction or in the direction of the fewest seam intersections.

Straight Set

Diagonal Set

1. Lay out the pieced blocks and alternate blocks (if you're using them) in diagonal rows. The edges of the quilt will be jagged at this point.

2. Add the side setting triangles and corner triangles to the layout. For the diagonally set projects in this book, the setting triangles are cut slightly oversized and trimmed after the quilt top is assembled.

3. To make sewing the rows less confusing, mark each row with a piece of paper and write the row number on each. The rows will include the side triangles.

4. With right sides together, sew the blocks in each row together. Press the seams in one direction. Press the seams in the next row in the opposite direction. Repeat for the remainder of the rows.

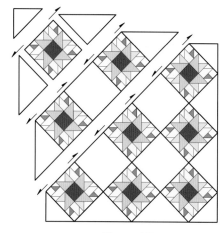

Diagonal Set

5. Lay out the rows and match up the seams. With right sides together, pin the blocks together at the intersecting seam allowances. Sew the rows together and press, alternating the direction of the seams.

6. Attach the four corner triangles and press the seams toward the triangles.

7. Using a long ruler for the sides and a square ruler for the corners, trim the excess fabric from the triangles, making sure to allow for a ¼" seam allowance all the way around the quilt top.

Mitered Borders

Directions are given with each project for measuring your quilt so you can cut borders to fit. However, if you're making mitered borders as in "Cross Your Heart" on page 49, you might want to follow the instructions below for making mitered borders that fit perfectly.

1. Estimate the finished outside dimensions of your quilt, including the borders. For example, if your quilt top measures 35½" x 50½" across the center and you want a 5"-wide border, your quilt will measure about 45" x 60" after the borders are attached. Add at least ½" to these measurements for seam allowances. To give yourself some leeway, you may want to add an additional 3" to 4" to those measurements. In this example, you would then cut two borders that measure approximately 48" long and two borders that measure approximately 63" long.

   Note: If your quilt has multiple borders, you can sew the individual border strips together first and treat the resulting unit as a single border. When mitering the corners, take care to match up the seam intersections of the multiple borders.

2. Fold the quilt in half and mark the centers of the quilt edges. Fold each border strip in half and mark the centers with pins.

3. Measure the length and width of the quilt top across the center. Note the measurements.

4. Place a pin at each end of the side border strips to mark the length of the quilt top. Repeat with the top and bottom borders.

Mark mid-point and ends.

5. Pin the borders to the quilt top, matching the centers. Line up the pins at either end of the border strip with the edges of the quilt. Stitch, beginning and ending the stitching ¼" from

the raw edges of the quilt top. Repeat with the remaining borders.

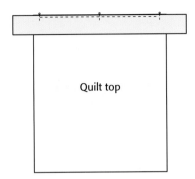

Quilt top

6. Lay the first corner to be mitered on the ironing board. Fold under one border strip at a 45° angle to the other strip. Press and pin.

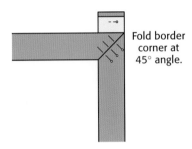

Fold border corner at 45° angle.

7. Fold the quilt with right sides together, lining up the adjacent edges of the border. If necessary, use a ruler and pencil to draw a line on the crease to make the stitching line more visible. Stitch on the pressed crease, sewing from the corner to the outside edges.

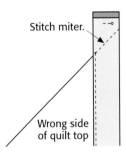

Stitch miter.

Wrong side of quilt top

8. Press the seam open, check the right side of the quilt to make sure the miters are neat, then turn over the quilt and trim away the excess border strips, leaving a ¼"-wide seam allowance.

9. Repeat with the remaining corners.

Sometimes I like to insert a folded flat piping into a seam to add a touch of color to the project. I find that using a printed fabric or one that reads as a solid is useful for separating a section of busy-looking patchwork from an equally busy-looking plaid border. If you've never used accent piping, I highly recommend trying it!

1. Cut enough 1"-wide strips to go around the perimeter of your quilt top or block that you want to accent. Sew the strips together end to end to make one continuous strip. Fold the strip in half lengthwise, wrong sides together, and press. From the long strip, cut pieces long enough to fit each side of the quilt top.

2. Attach the folded piping to the edge of the quilt top by aligning the raw edges of the piping with the raw edges of the quilt. Make sure the folded edge of the piping is facing toward the inside of the quilt top. Machine baste the piping in place, using a scant ¼" seam allowance. Using a basting stitch will make it easier to remove these stitches in case they show after adding the border.

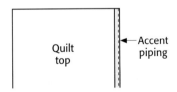

Quilt top

← Accent piping

3. Attach the border in the usual fashion, remembering to reset the machine stitch length to normal. Press all seams toward the border, but leave the flap of piping pressed toward the interior of the quilt.

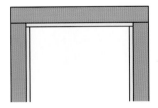

Finishing Your Quilt

If you're like most quilters, once you're finished piecing your quilt top, you'll experience a great sense of satisfaction. Then you'll face the reality that you still need to quilt and bind it before it's really finished. There are lots of books available on quilting techniques, but I'll give you some pointers on getting ready to quilt and attaching the binding to your project.

Quilt Backing

In the project directions, you'll find the amount of yardage you need to back your quilt. For small projects, one width of fabric is sufficient, but if your quilt top is wider or longer than 40", you'll need to piece two or more sections of fabric together to make a backing large enough for your quilt.

1. Measure the quilt top. You'll need to add 6" to the width and length of these measurements to determine how big your quilt backing needs to be. This will give you extra fabric on all edges for the quilting process, because sometimes the layers can shift slightly and you don't want to run short of fabric.

2. If you need to piece the backing, I recommend seaming it so that a seam does not run up the middle of the quilt back. This is typically where quilts are folded for storage, and the fold will put stress on the seam. You can either piece the backing with one large panel and one narrow one for an off-center seam, or if you need two full widths of fabric, you can cut one in half vertically and then sew a half panel to each side of the full-width panel. Press the seams to one side.

One fabric width

Partial fabric width

3. Layer the backing, right side down, on a table or floor, then place the batting on top of it, and the quilt top, right side up, on top of that. Baste the layers together for quilting. You may want to baste with safety pins for machine quilting (they're easy to remove when you are stitching), or with thread for hand quilting.

Binding

Most quilters are familiar with straight-grain binding. It's quick and easy to cut and sew and makes efficient use of your fabric. But sometimes a quilt calls for bias binding. Why? Sometimes it's for a practical reason, such as the quilt "Cherry Squares" (page 56) that has curved edges. The bias binding eases nicely around the curves without puckering. Sometimes bias binding is merely an aesthetic choice. Plaids cut on the bias are more dynamic than those cut on the straight grain when used for binding. Bias binding allows you to see all parts of a plaid rather than the same stripe all the way around the quilt. If you've never made bias binding, making one for a plaid quilt is a great time to start.

Making Bias Binding

1. Determine the grain of the piece of fabric (parallel to the selvage edges) and then fold the fabric to form a 45° angle.

2. Trim off the fold, using a long ruler and a rotary cutter.

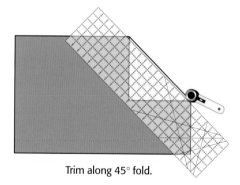

Trim along 45° fold.

3. Working from this bias-cut edge, measure and cut bias strips to your desired width. Cut strips 2" wide for a ¼" finished binding, or cut them 2½" wide for a ½" finished binding.

4. Sew the strips together end to end to make one continuous strip that is long enough to extend around the entire perimeter of the quilt.

5. Fold the strip in half lengthwise with the wrong sides together and press the fold in place.

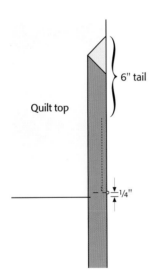

Attaching Binding

Many quilters attach binding using a folded miter corner. I like to stitch the mitered corners in place. Here's how to do just that.

1. Align the raw edges of the binding with the raw edges of the quilt (with the folded edge of the binding facing toward the center of the quilt). Sew the binding to the quilt with a ¼" seam allowance. Stop sewing ¼" from the corner and backstitch. Remove the quilt from the machine.

6" tail

Quilt top

¼"

2. Fold the edge of the quilt under and out of the way. Then fold the loose end of the binding to the back of the quilt, leaving ½" between where you stopped stitching and the fold for 2½"-wide binding. (For 2"-wide binding, leave ⅜"

from the stopping point to the fold.) Sew an inverted V in the binding as shown and backstitch at both the beginning and the end. The stitching should start and stop ¼" from the edge of the binding, but the point of the inverted V should be exactly at the fold. Remove the quilt from the machine.

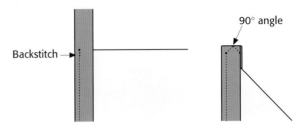

90° angle

Backstitch

3. Fold the length of binding toward the already-sewn seam and align the raw edges of the binding with the next edge of the quilt top. Start sewing at the ¼" point from the corner. Repeat the process for each corner.

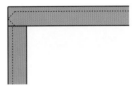

4. On the last side of the quilt, stop stitching about 7" from where you began. Overlap the ending tail with the starting tail. Trim the binding ends with a perpendicular cut so the overlap is exactly the same distance as the cut width of your binding strips. (If your binding strips are 2½" wide, the overlap should be 2½"; for 2"-wide binding, the overlap should be 2".)

2½" overlap

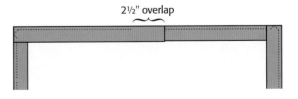

5. Open up the two ends of the folded binding. Place the tails right sides together so they join to form a right angle as shown. Pin the binding tails together, then mark a diagonal stitching line from corner to corner.

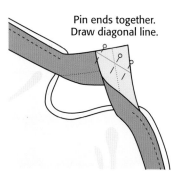

Pin ends together.
Draw diagonal line.

6. Stitch the binding tails together on the marked line. Trim the seam allowance to ¼"; press the seam open to reduce bulk. Refold the binding, align the edges with the raw edges of the quilt top, and finish sewing it in place.

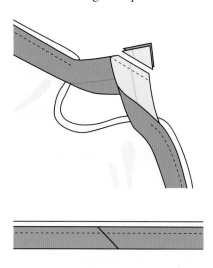

7. Trim the seam allowances at the corners and then turn the binding to the back of the quilt. Blindstitch the binding in place. Notice how the miters are already finished!

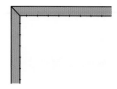

Adding a Hanging Sleeve

Several of the quilts in this book are wall hangings. To make it easy to display them, add a hanging sleeve to the finished quilt.

1. Using leftover fabric from the quilt backing, cut a strip 6" to 8" wide and 1" shorter than the width of your quilt. Fold the ends under ½", then again ½" to make a hem. Stitch in place.

2. Fold the fabric strip in half lengthwise, wrong sides together, and baste the raw edges to the top of the quilt back. The top edge of the sleeve will be secured when the binding is sewn onto the quilt.

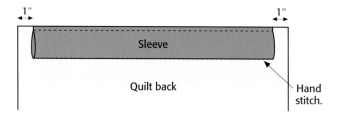

1"   1"

Sleeve

Quilt back   Hand
                                                    stitch.

3. Finish the sleeve after the binding has been attached by blindstitching the bottom of the sleeve in place. Push the bottom edge of the sleeve up just a bit to provide a little give so the hanging rod does not put strain on the quilt.

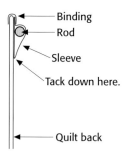

Binding
Rod
Sleeve
Tack down here.

Quilt back

Signing Your Quilt

Future generations will be interested to know more than just who made the quilt and when, so be sure to include the name of the quilt, your name, your city and state, the date, the name of the recipient if the quilt is a gift, and any other interesting or important information about the quilt. The information can be handwritten, typed, or embroidered.

Stitch Dictionary

The following appliqué and embroidery stitches are useful for some of the projects in this book.

Blanket Stitch

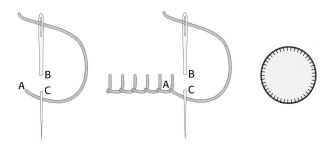

Blind Stitch

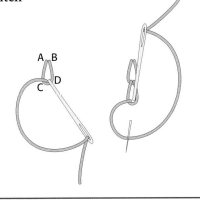

Chain Stitch

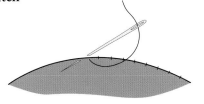

French Knot

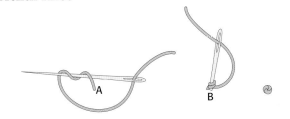

Running Stitch

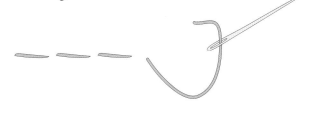

Satin Stitch

Stem Stitch

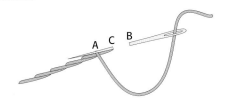

About the Author

©Jurick

Debbie Bacon is a fourth-generation Oklahoman. She graduated from the University of Oklahoma in 1973 with a degree in Fashion Arts. After many years of working in broadcasting, business, and public relations, Debbie "retired" to raise a family. She and her husband, Ron, have three children. In 1985 she took her first quilting class and has been hooked ever since. She has won many awards for her work and enjoys the creative challenge that quilting offers.

Debbie is an active member of the American Quilter's Society, the Green Country Quilt Guild in Tulsa, the Central Oklahoma Quilt Guild, and has chartered other groups, including the Oklahoma Quilter's State Organization, of which she is a former president. She regularly lectures and teaches classes on a variety of quiltmaking techniques. Debbie currently designs and produces quilt patterns under the Bacon Bit 'N Pieces label.